Hello!
Ever since I was young,
I remember wanting to
draw ALL the time.
As I grew, so did the
passion and intrest of
seeing stories come to life
through video games.
These pieces I've made
are all made with that
love and passion.
From creepy to cute,
I hope you enjoy!

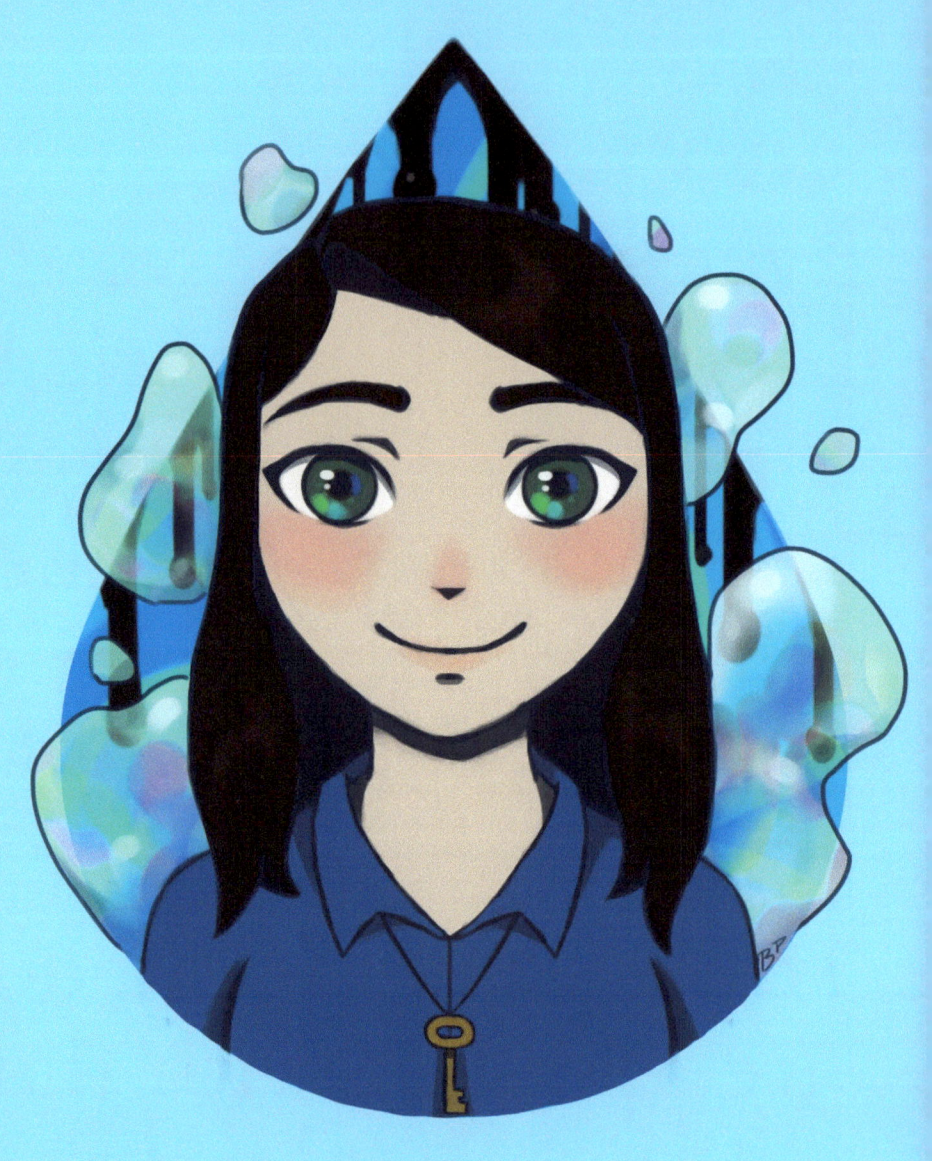

(It's me!)

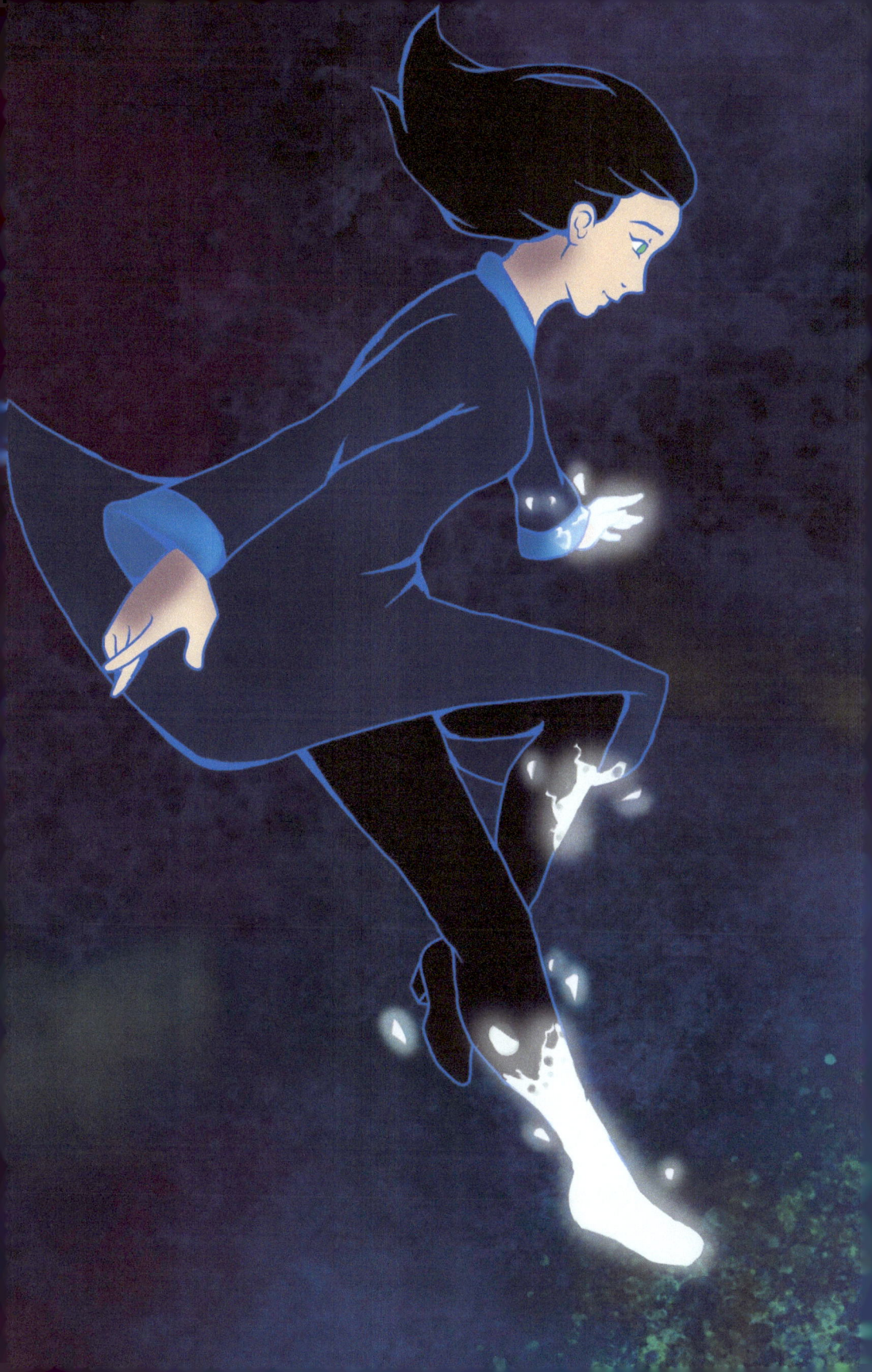

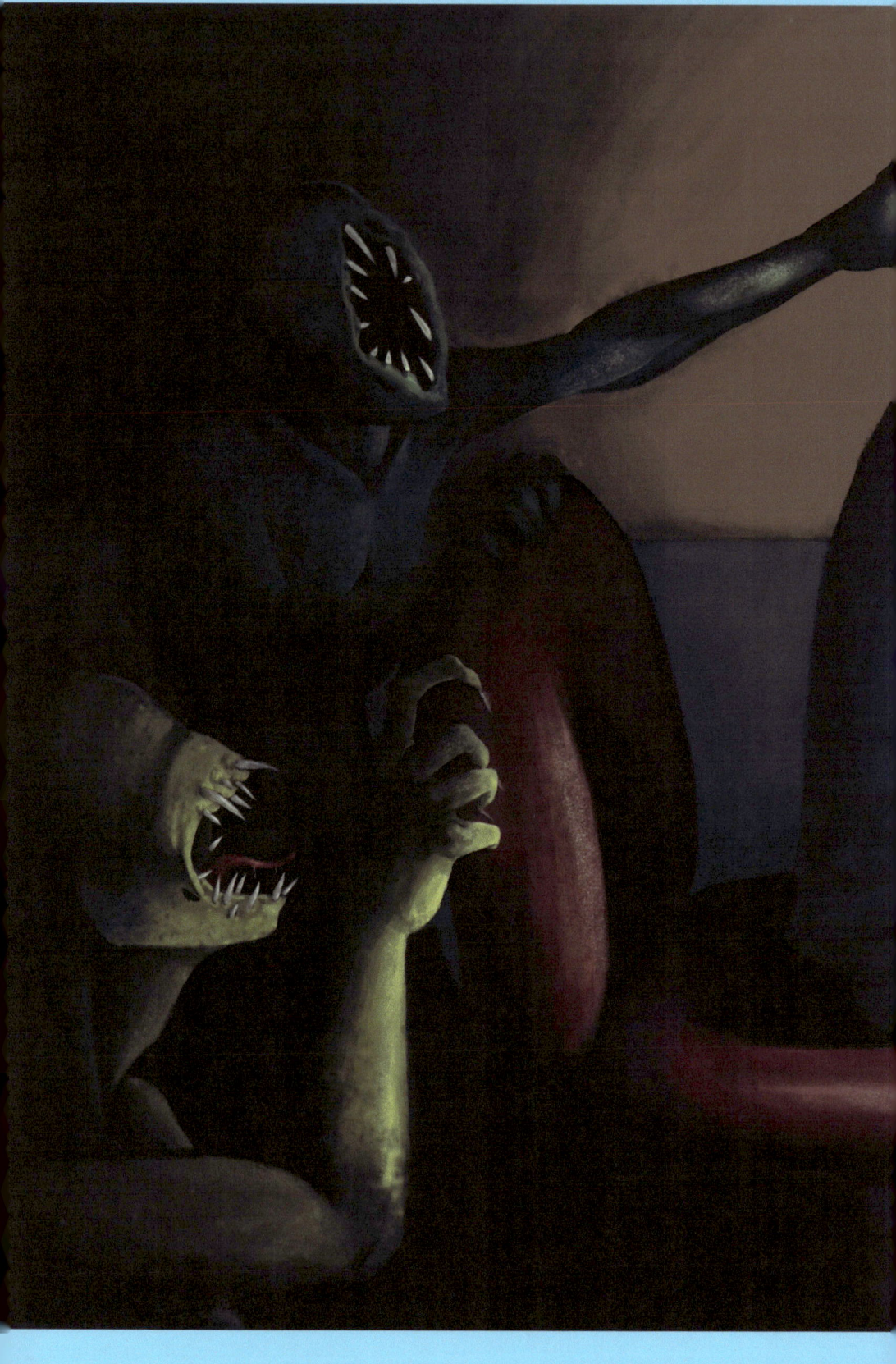

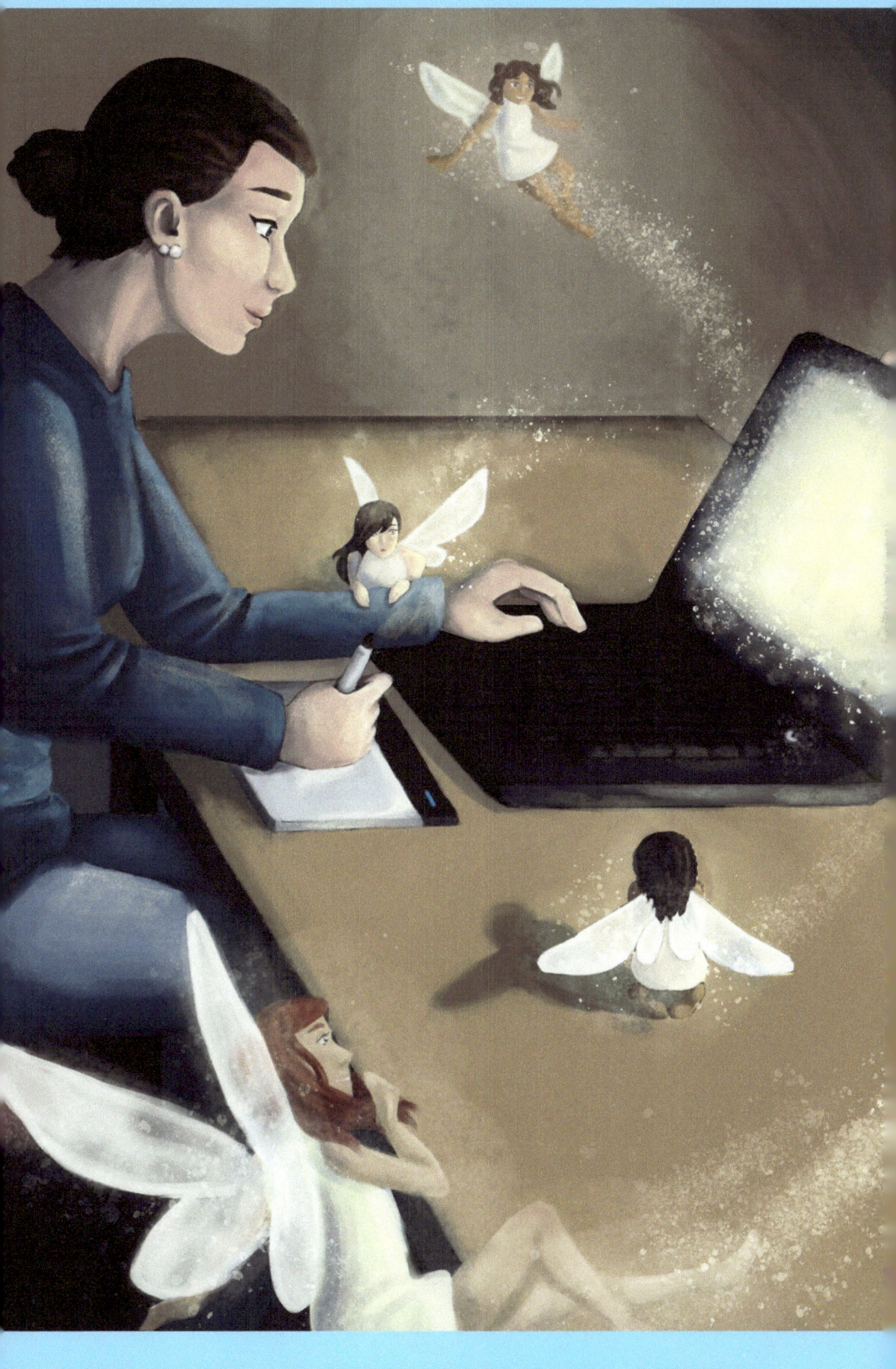

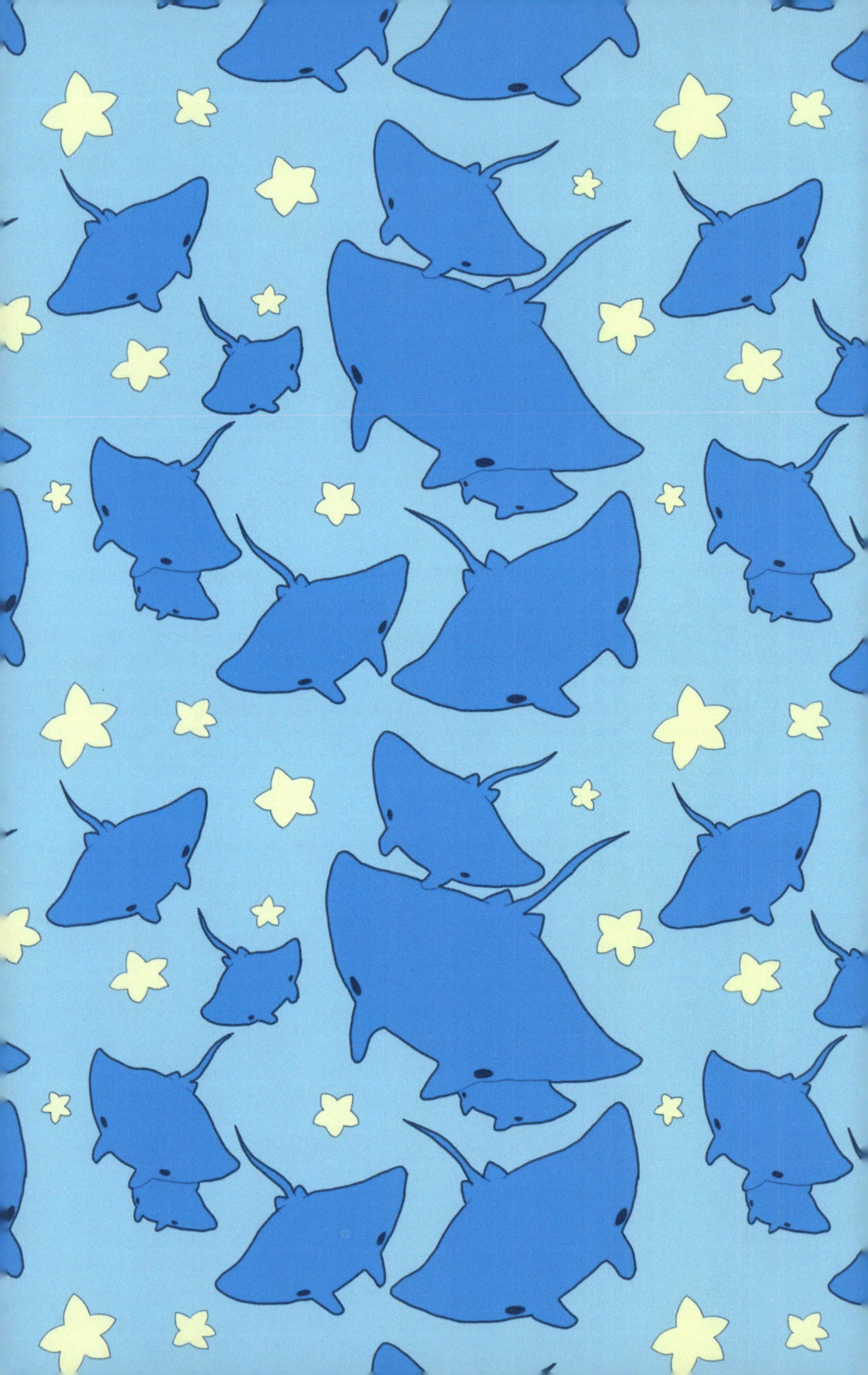

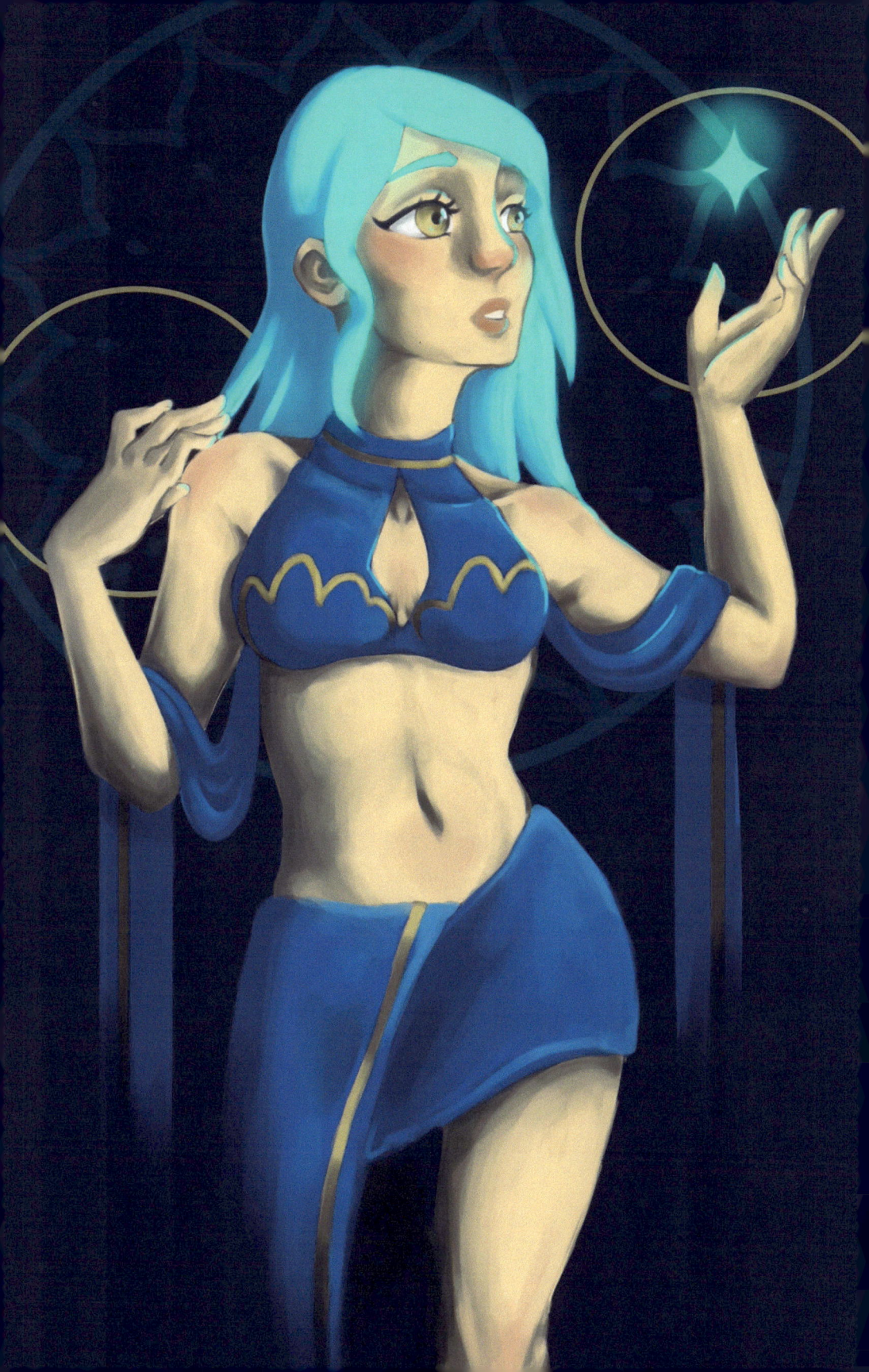

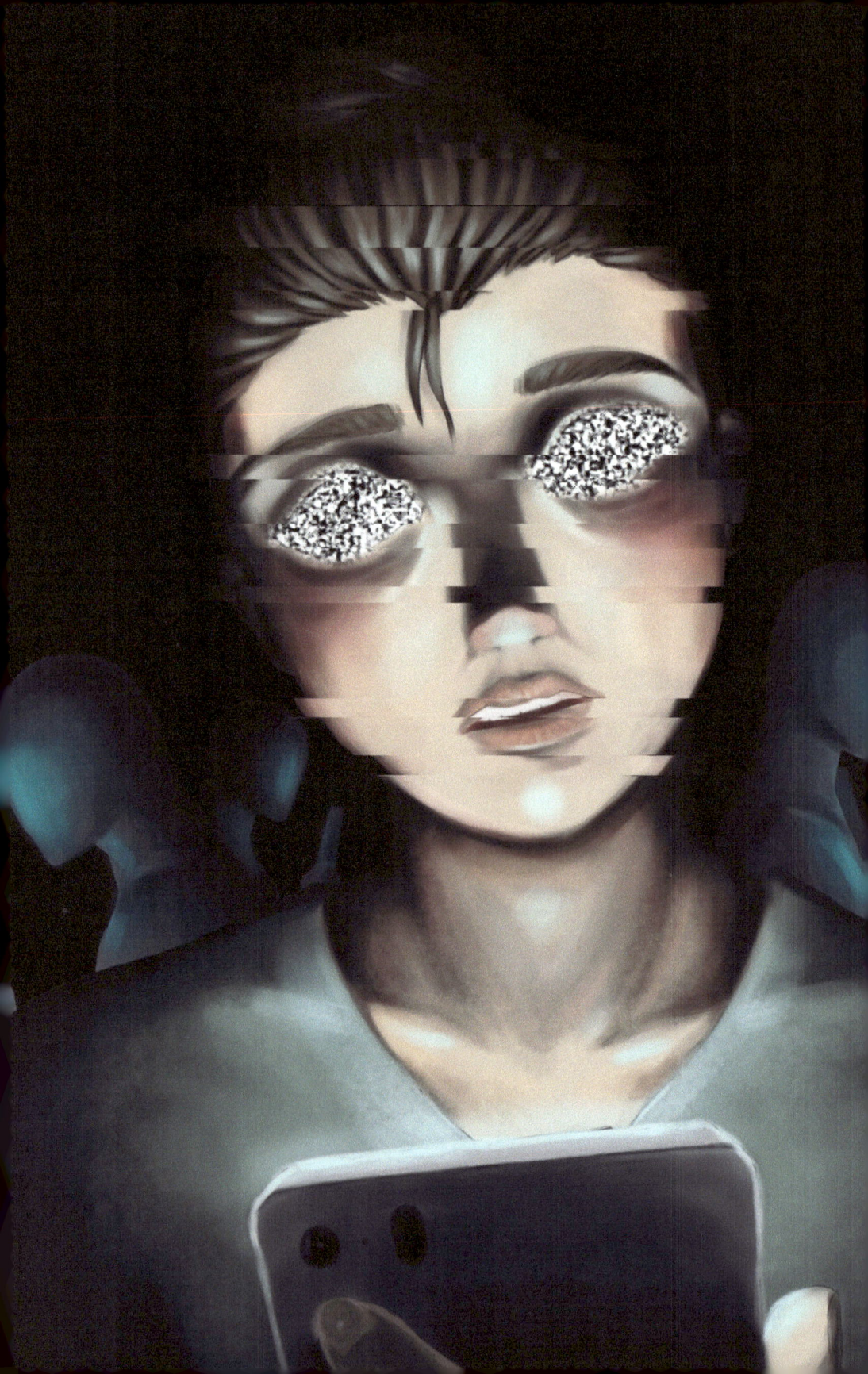

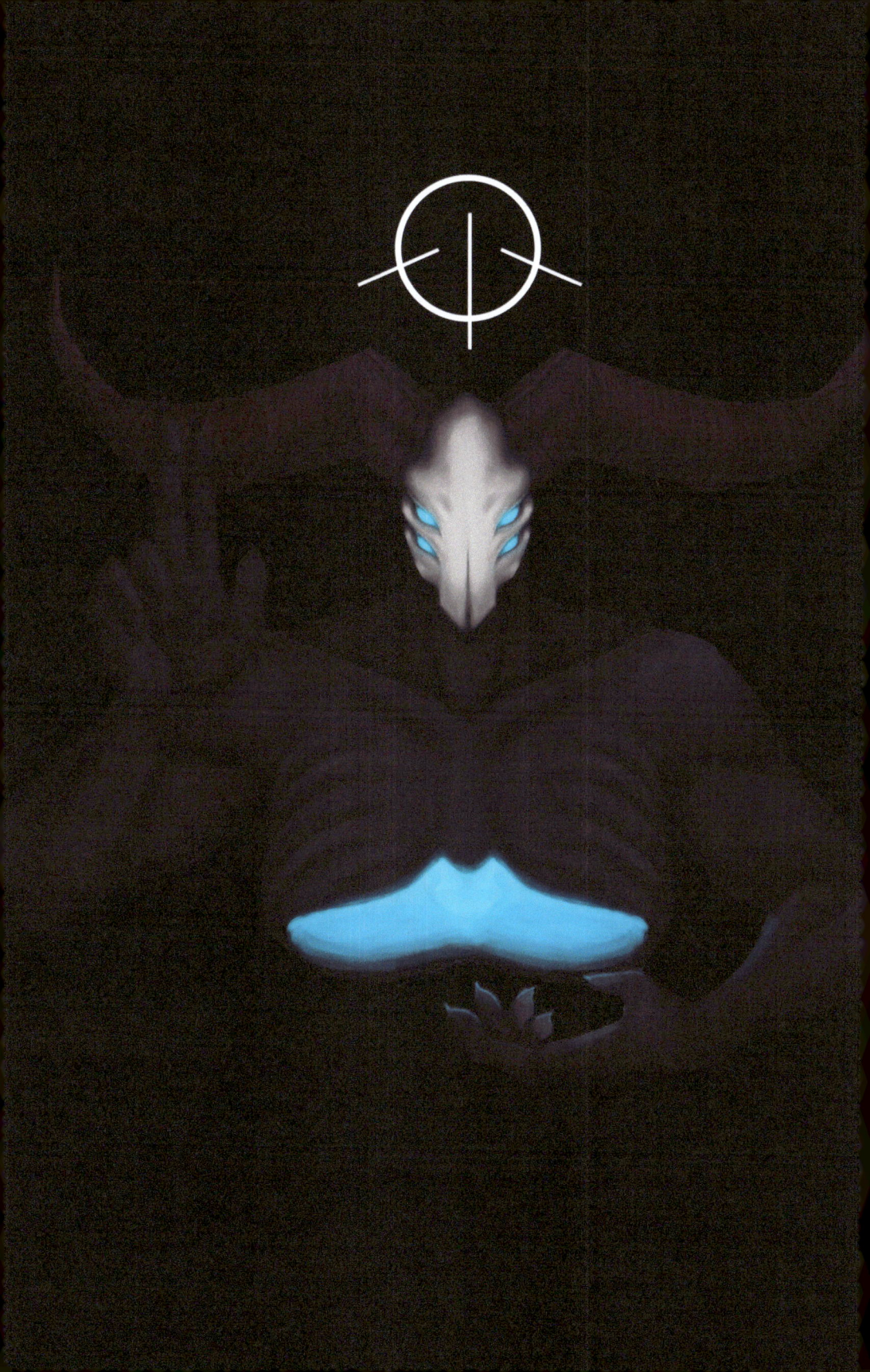

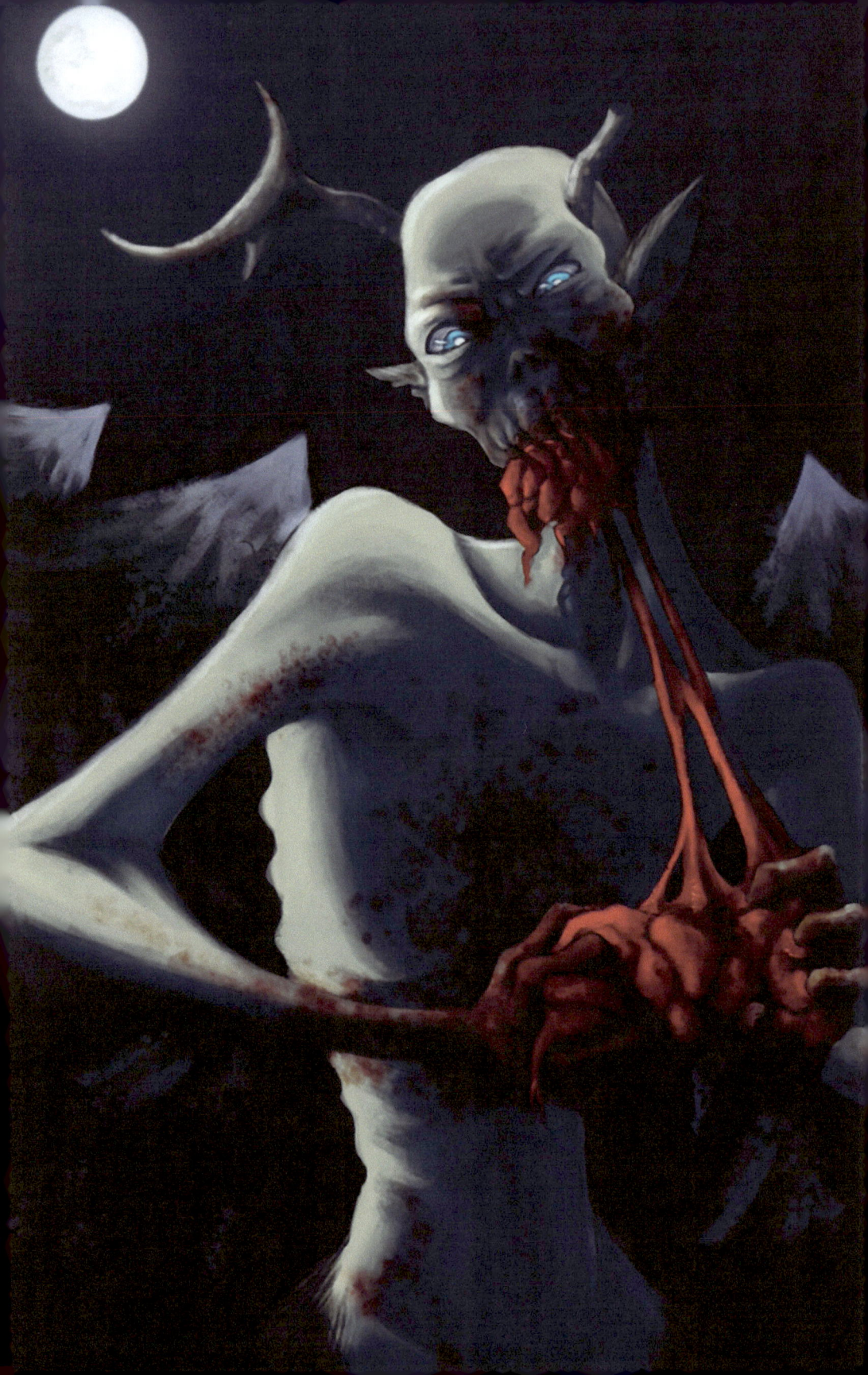

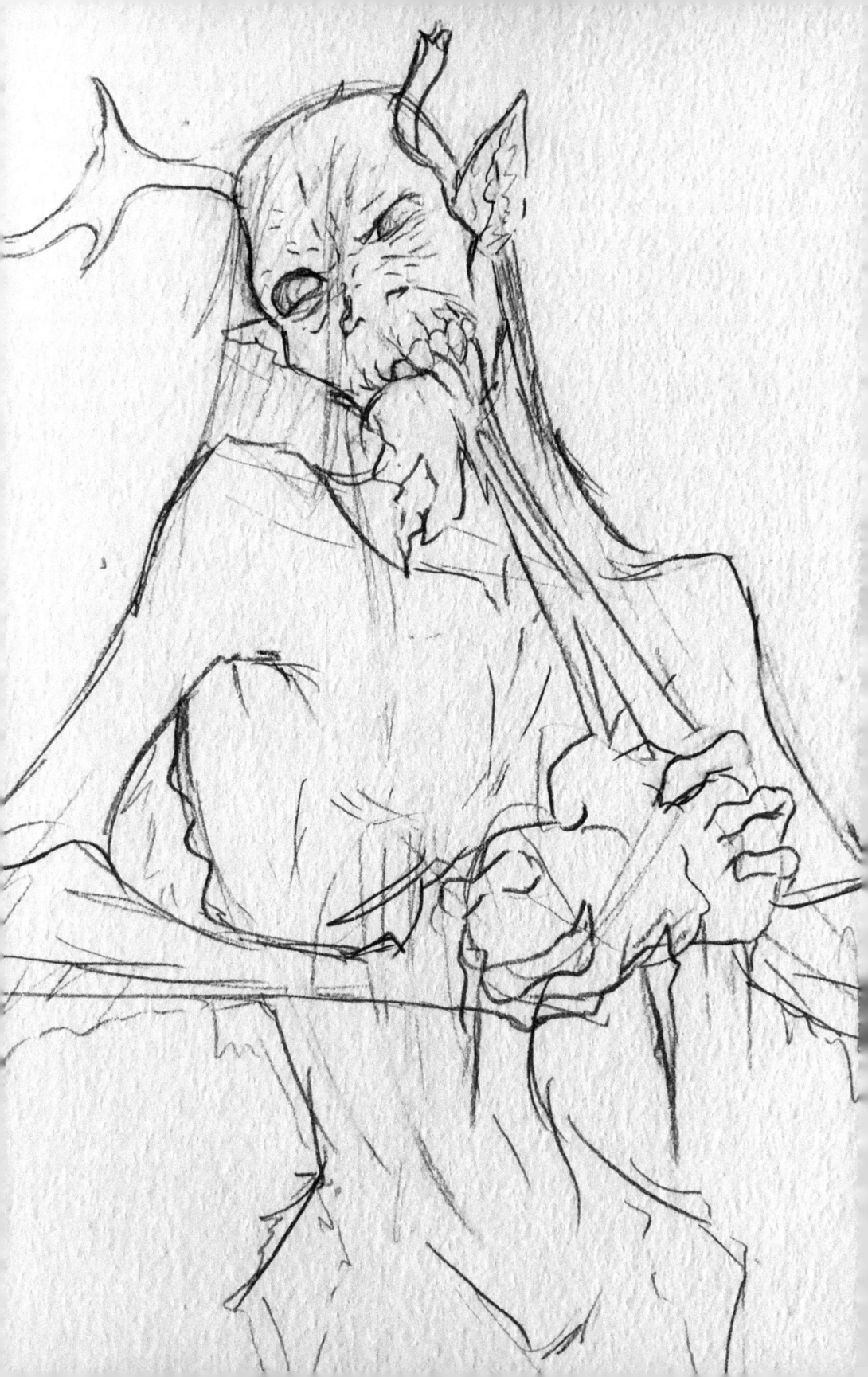

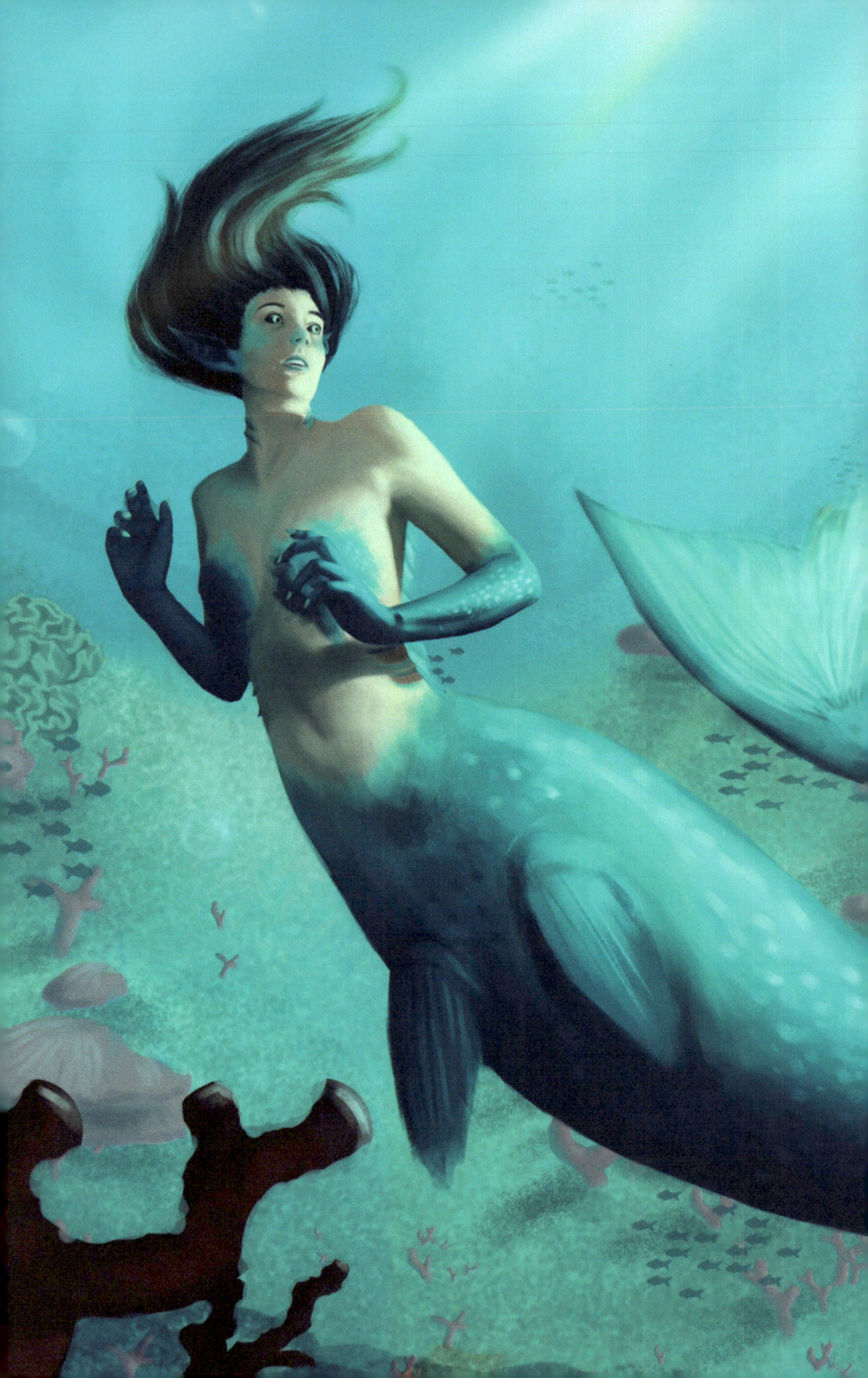

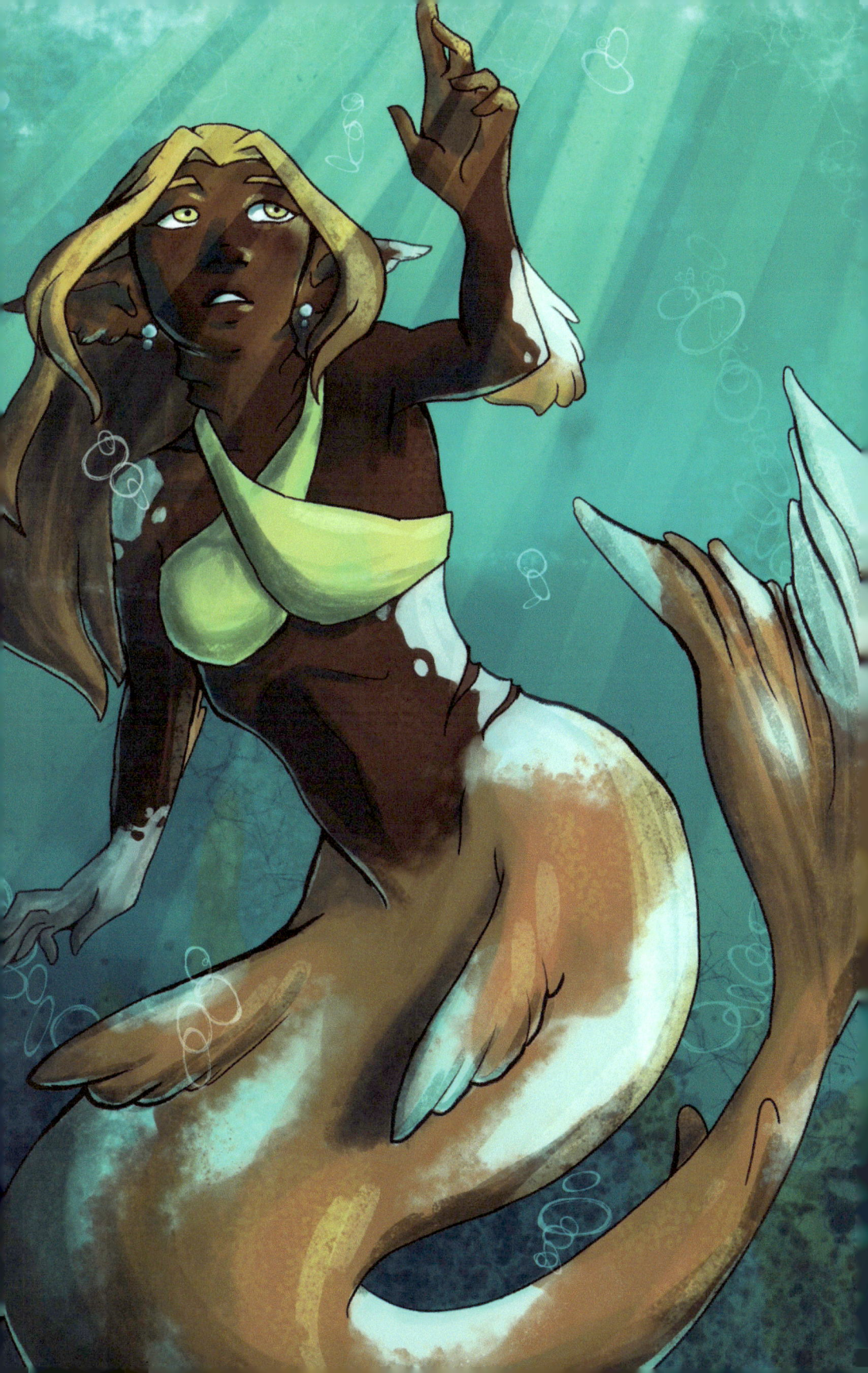

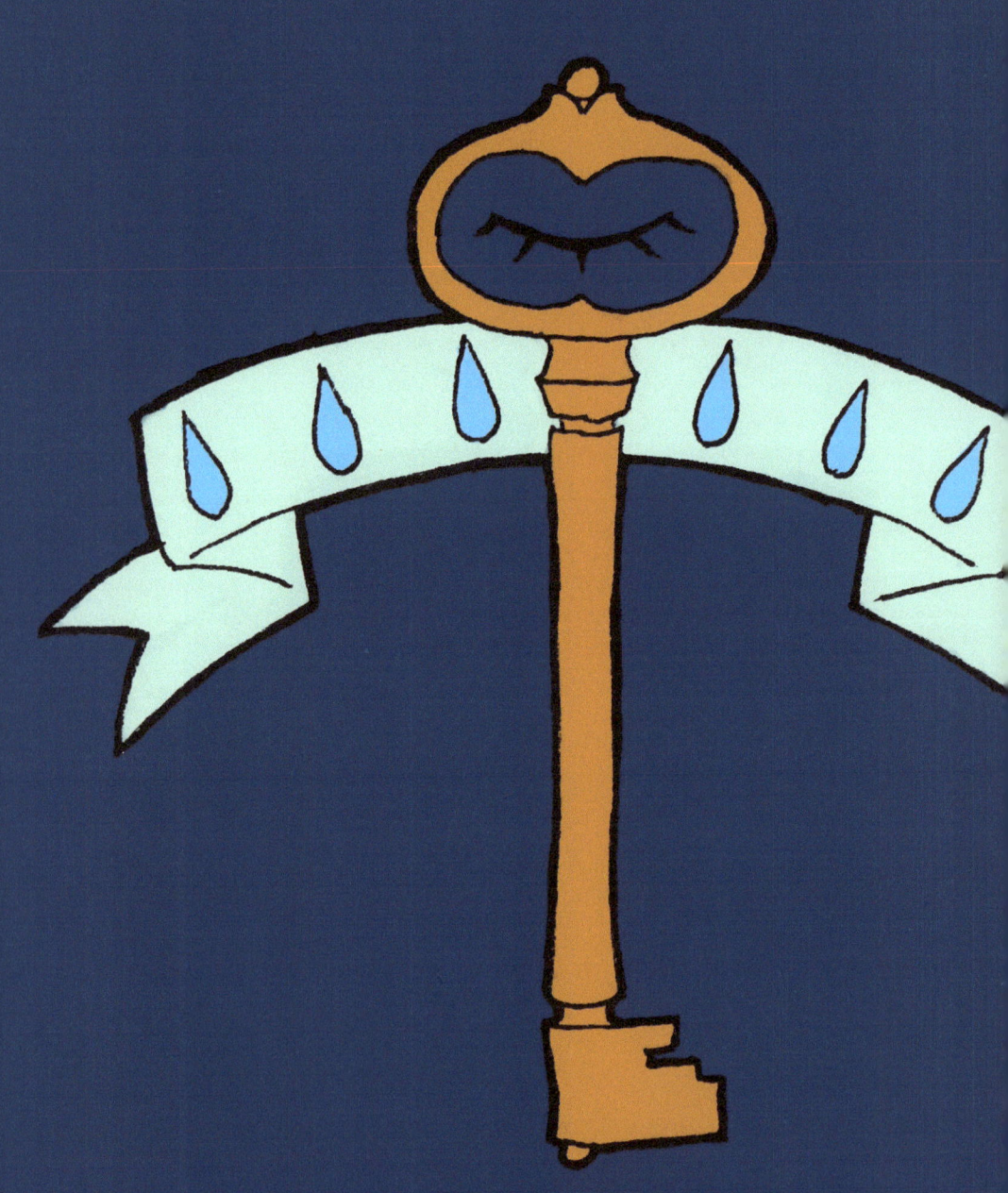

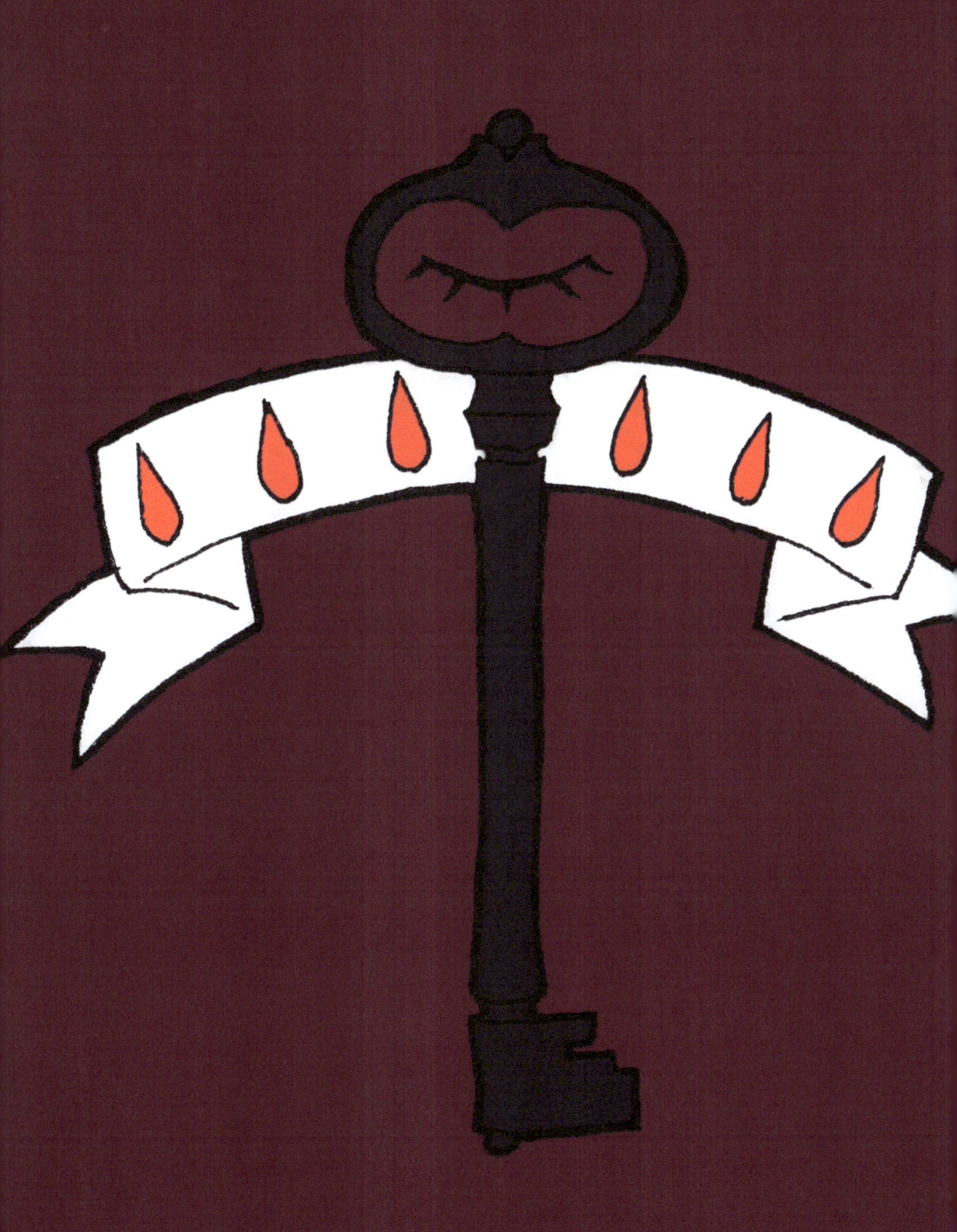

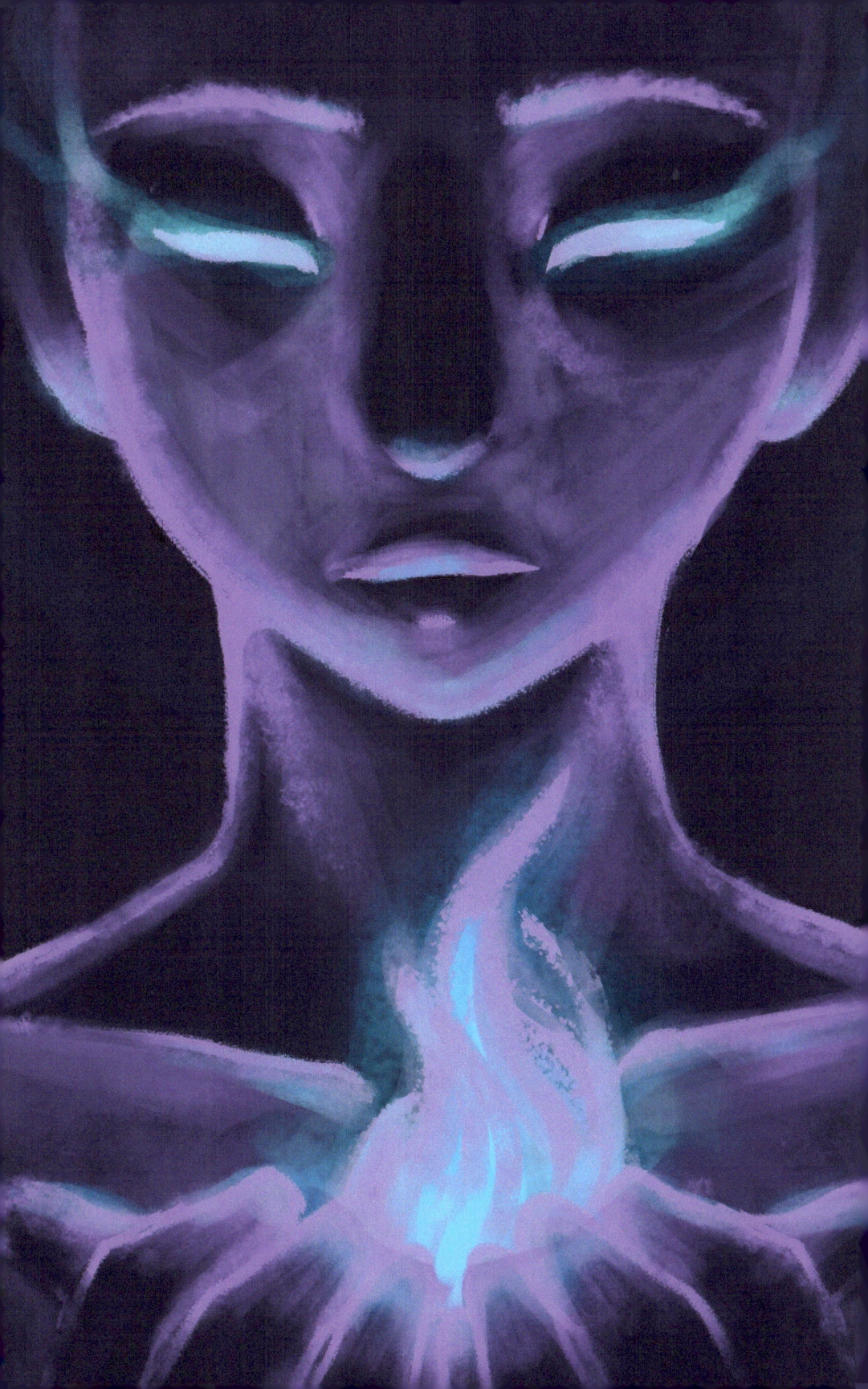

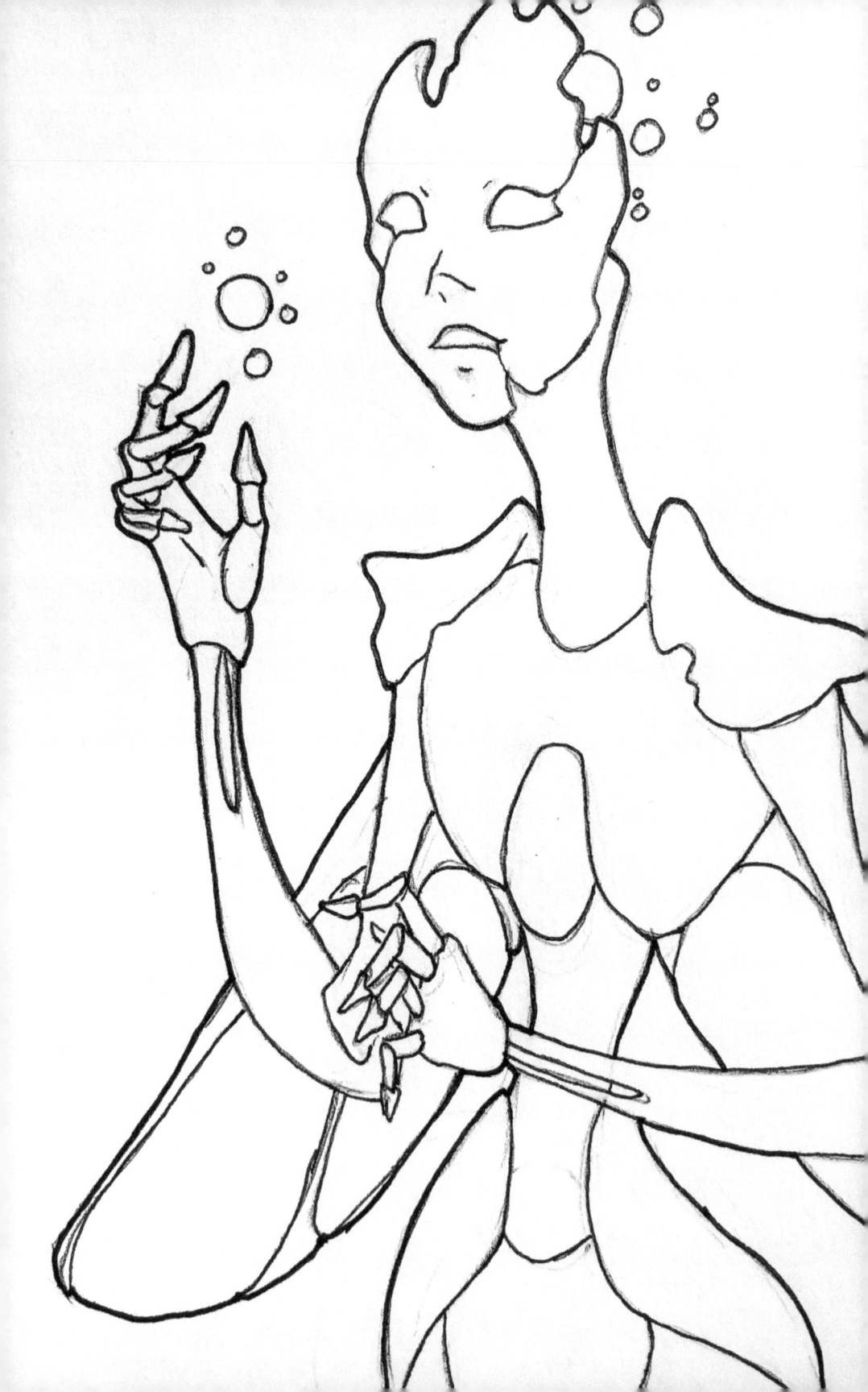

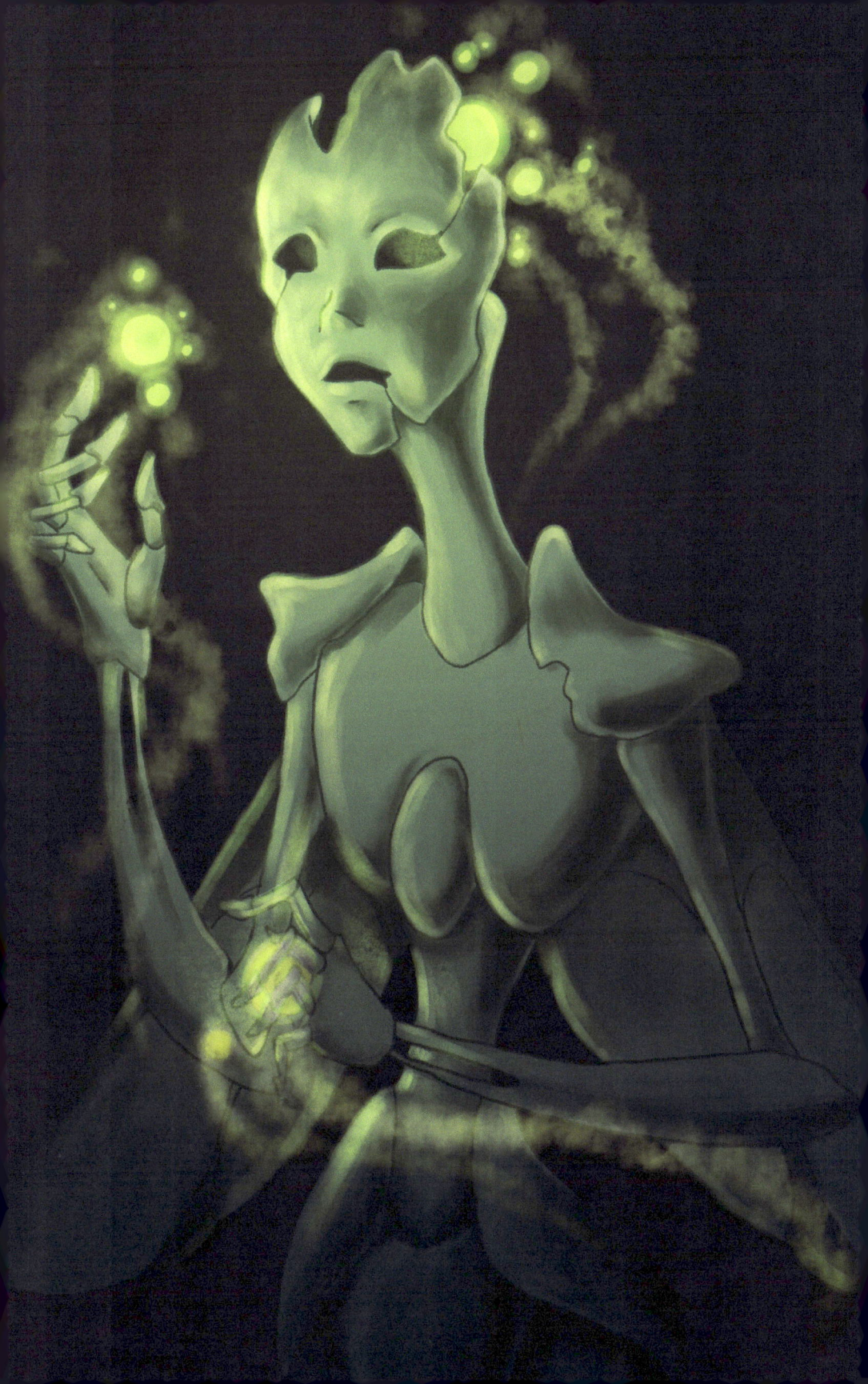

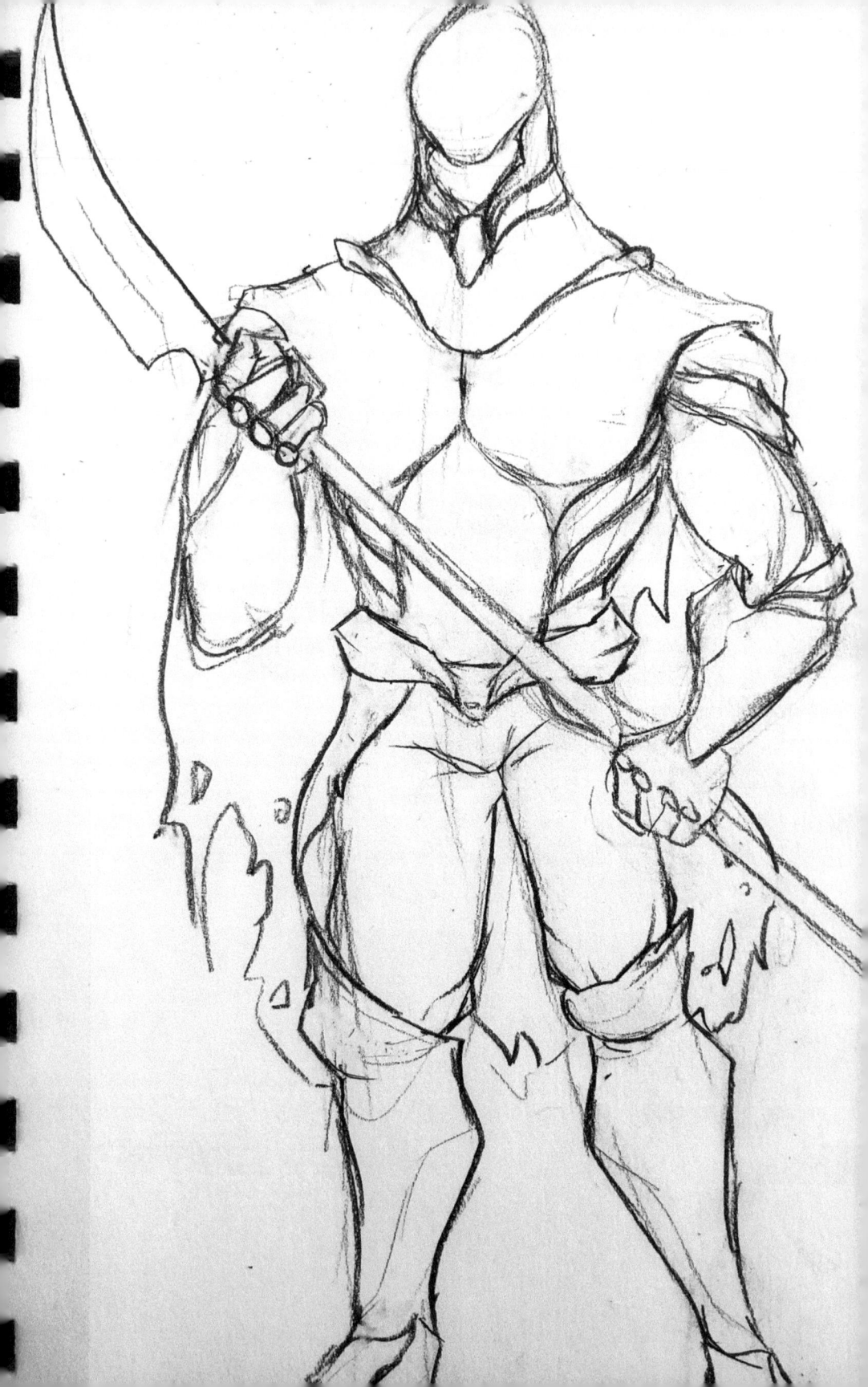

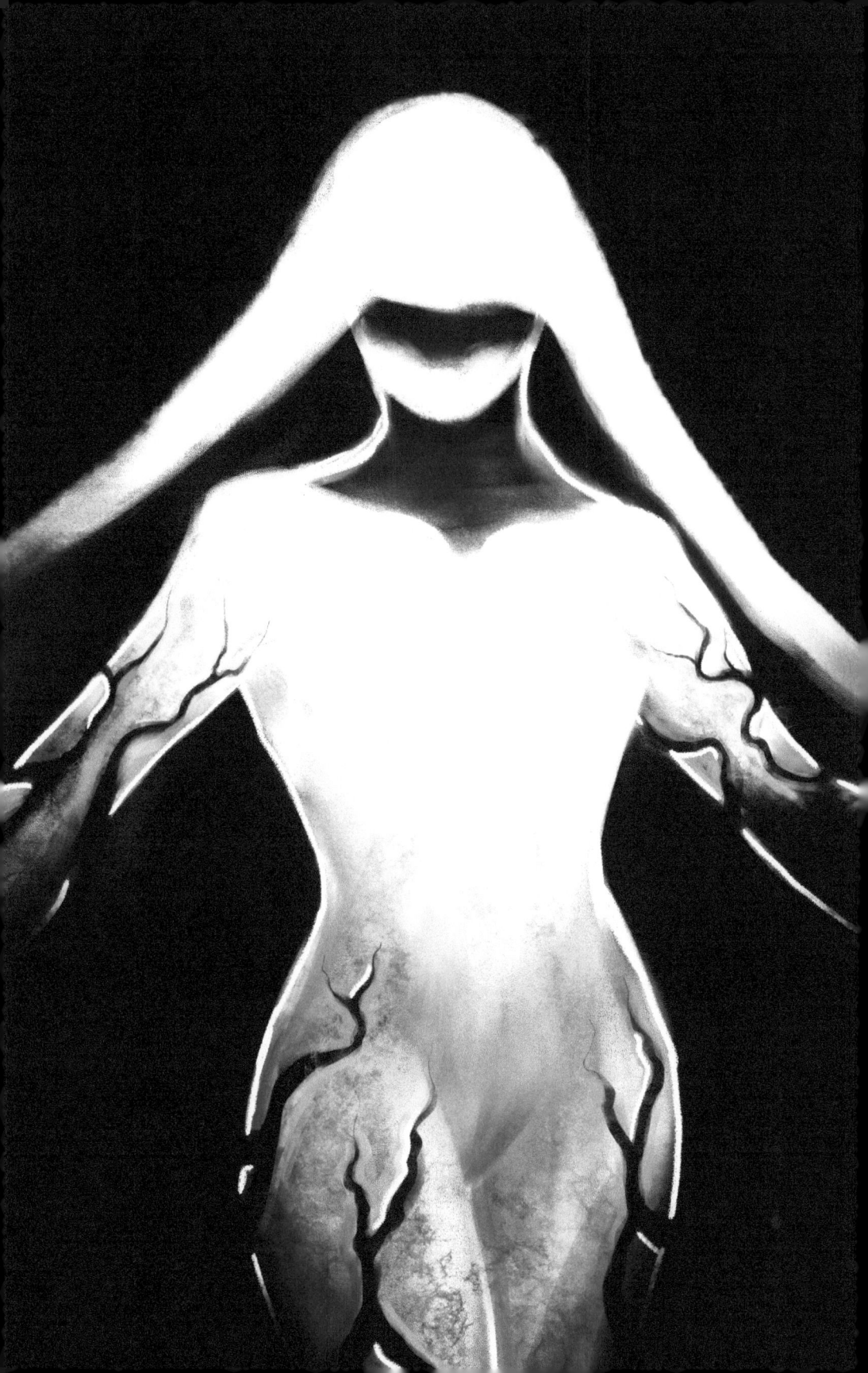

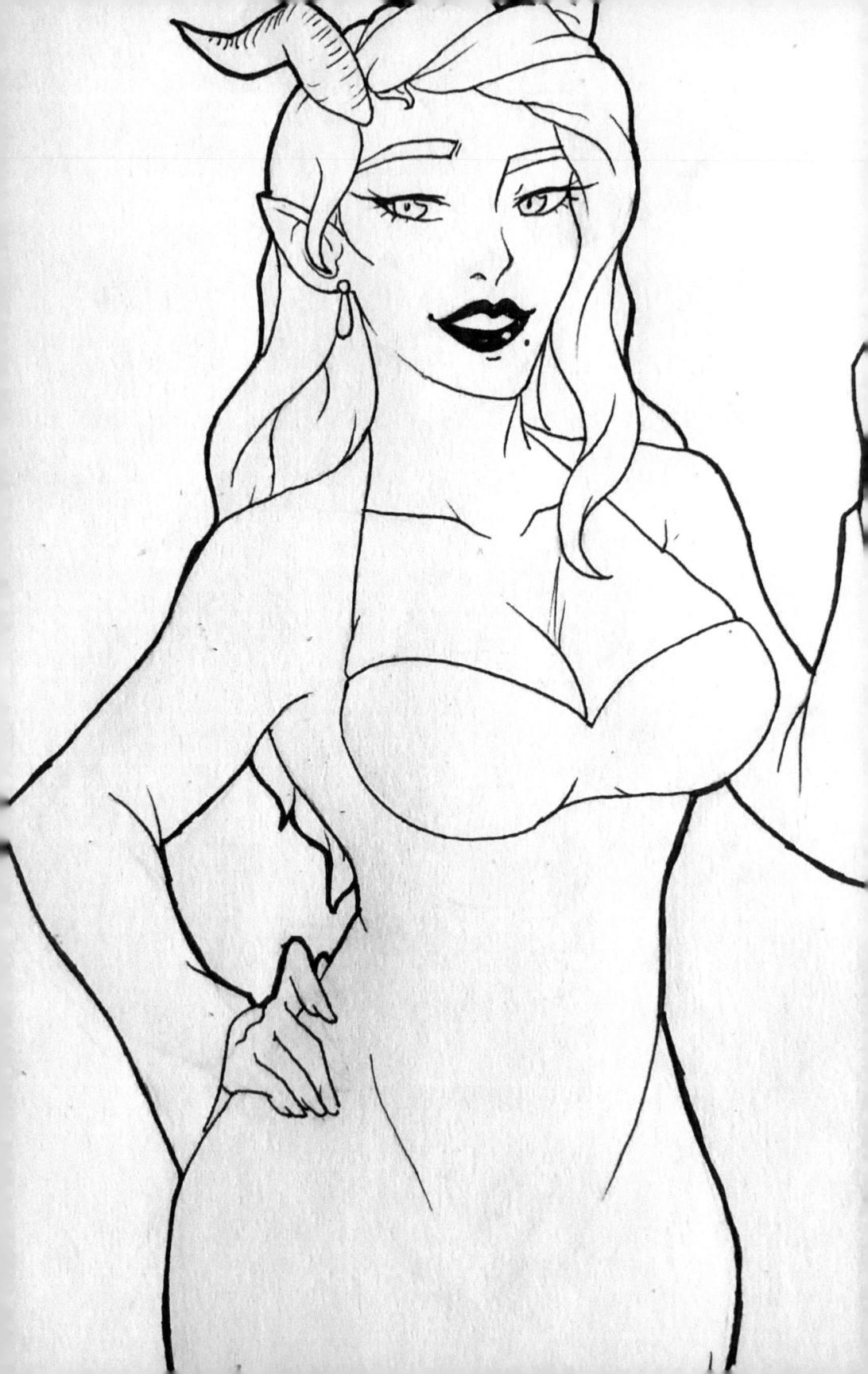

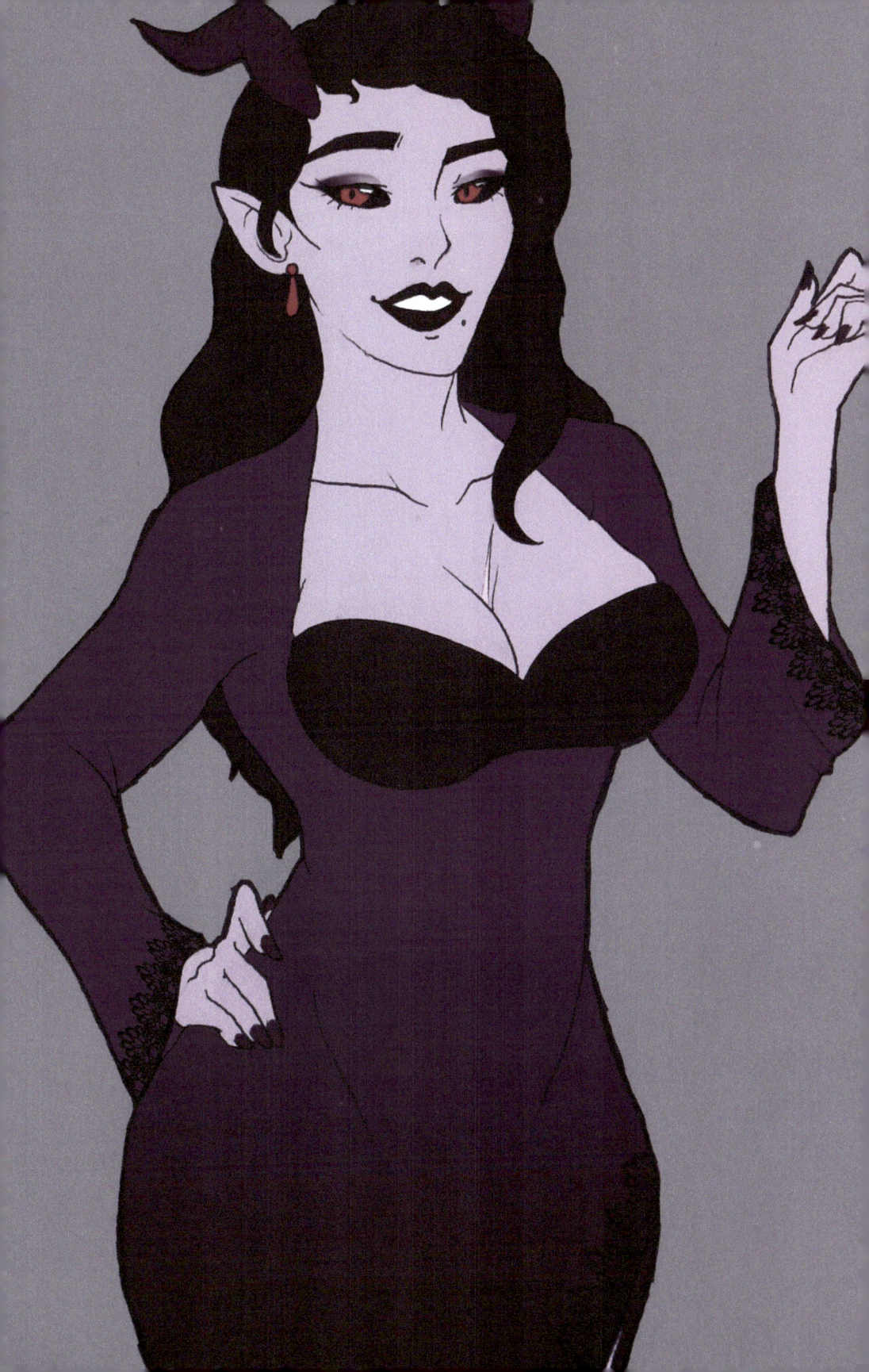

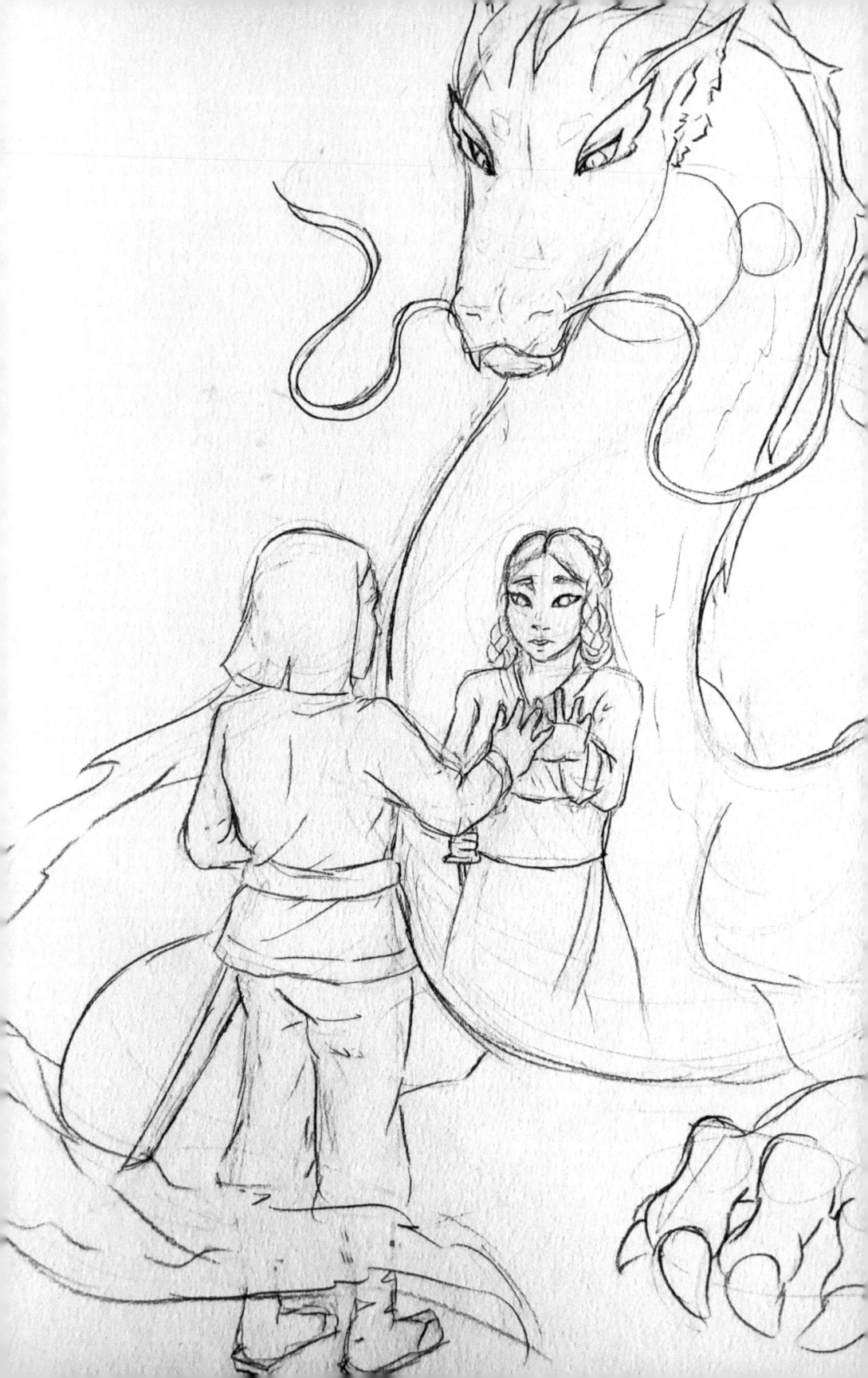

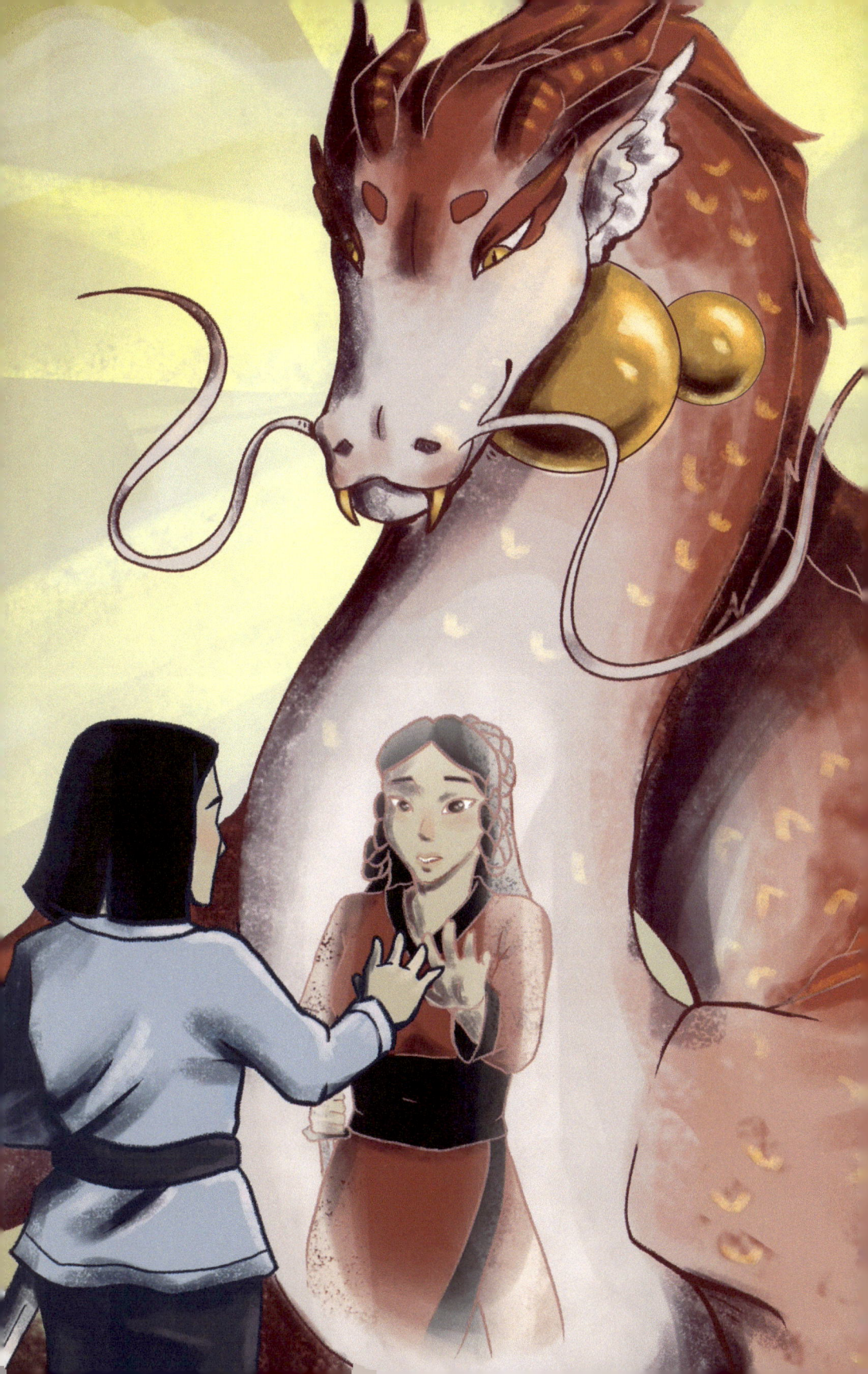

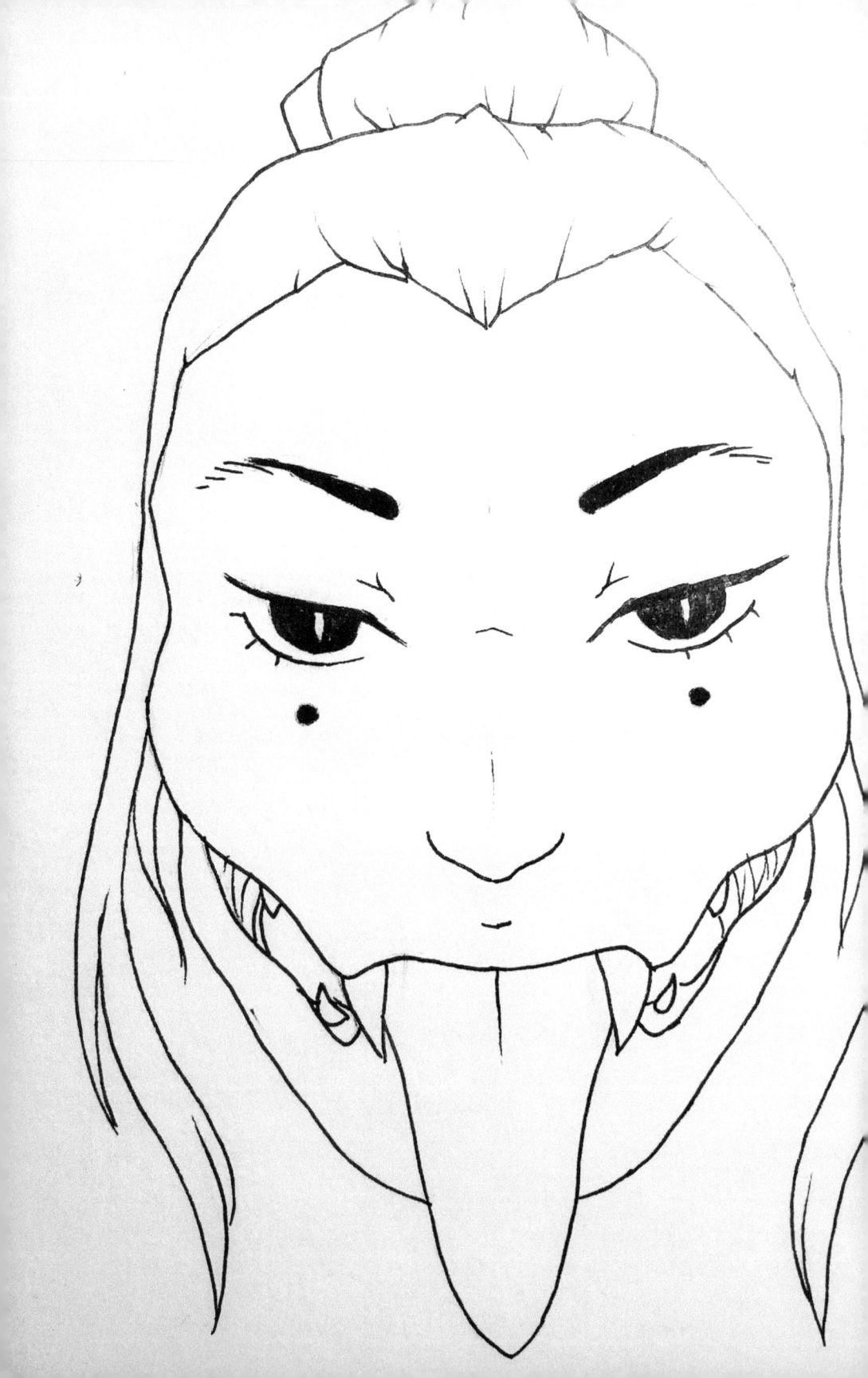

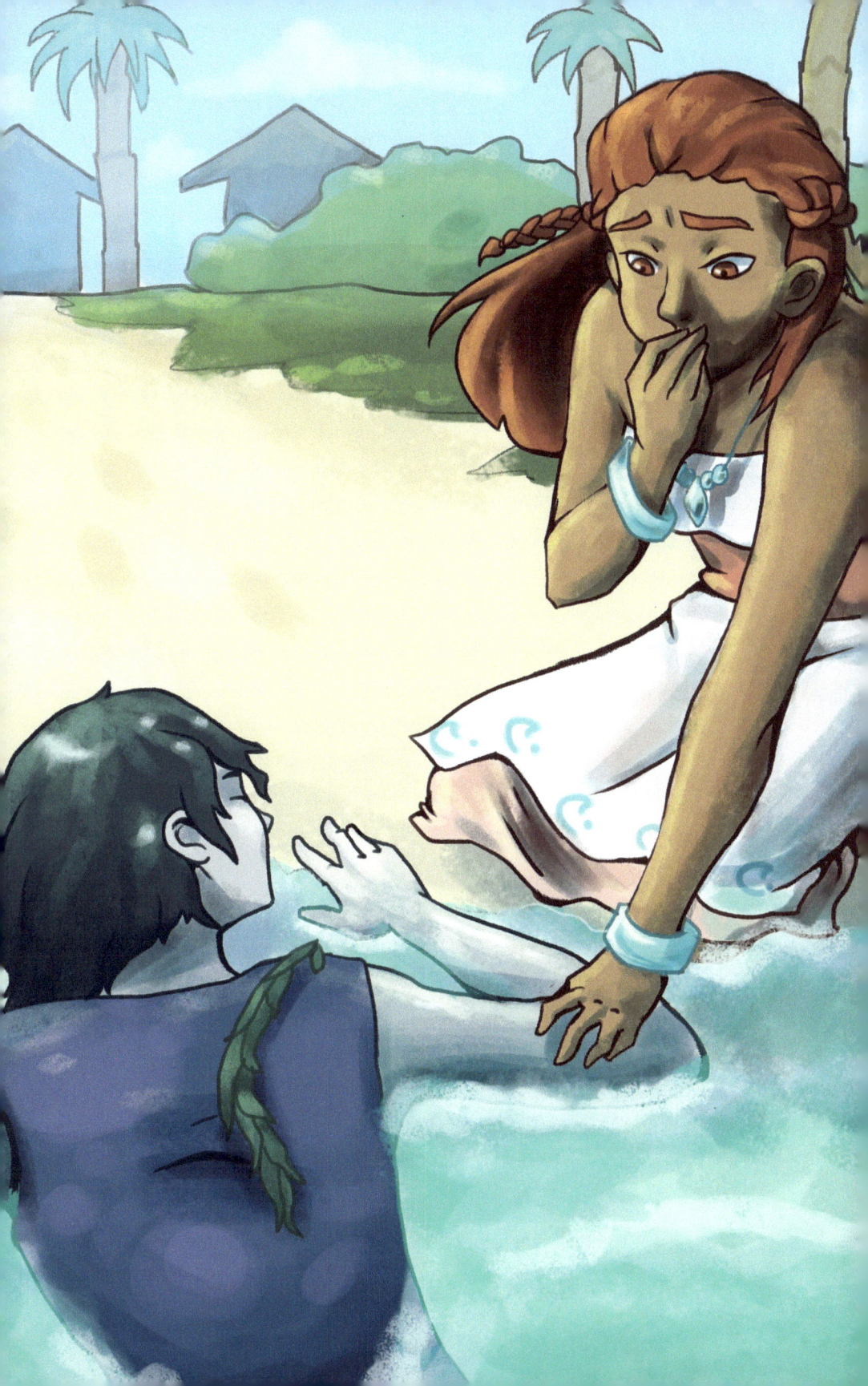

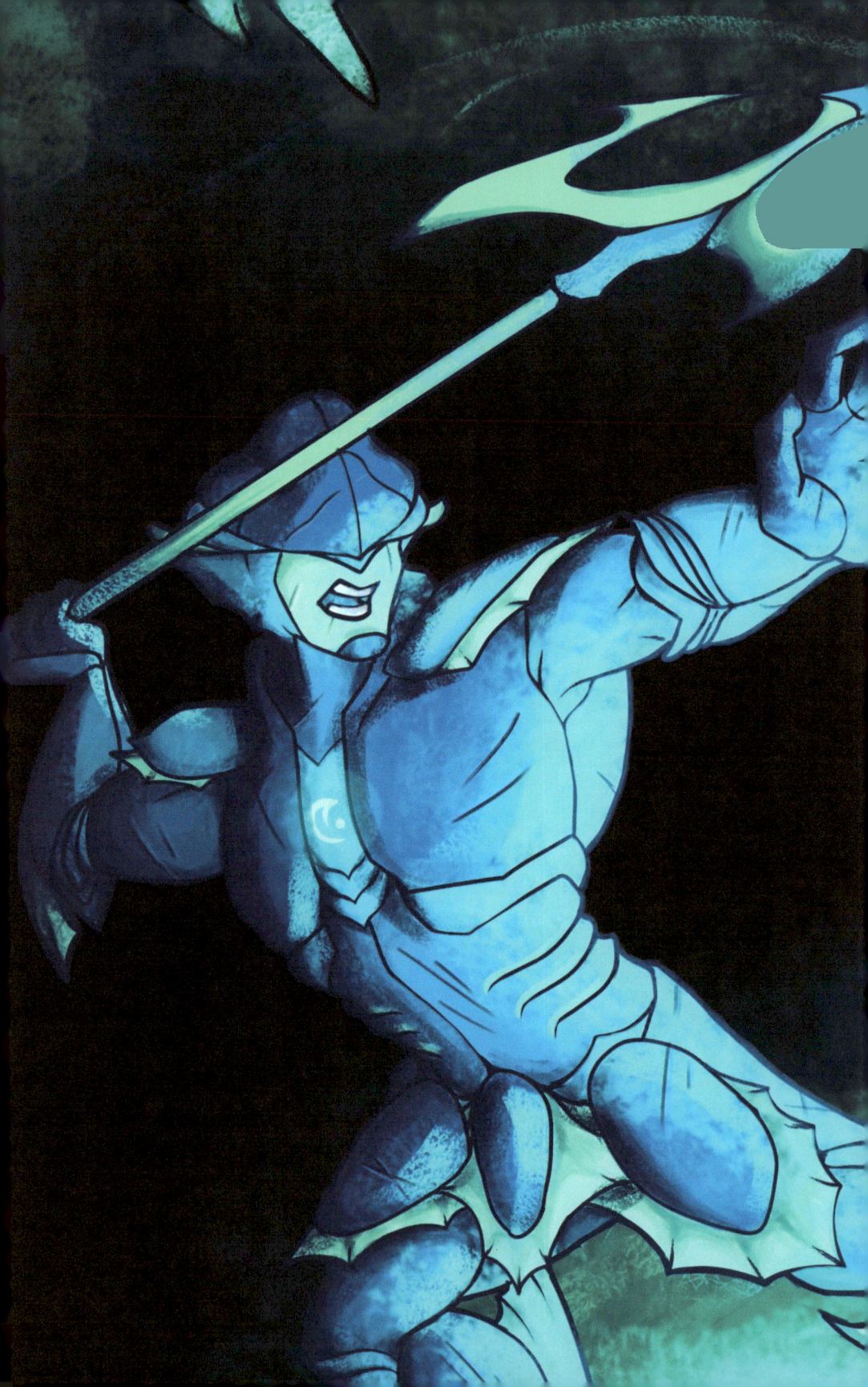

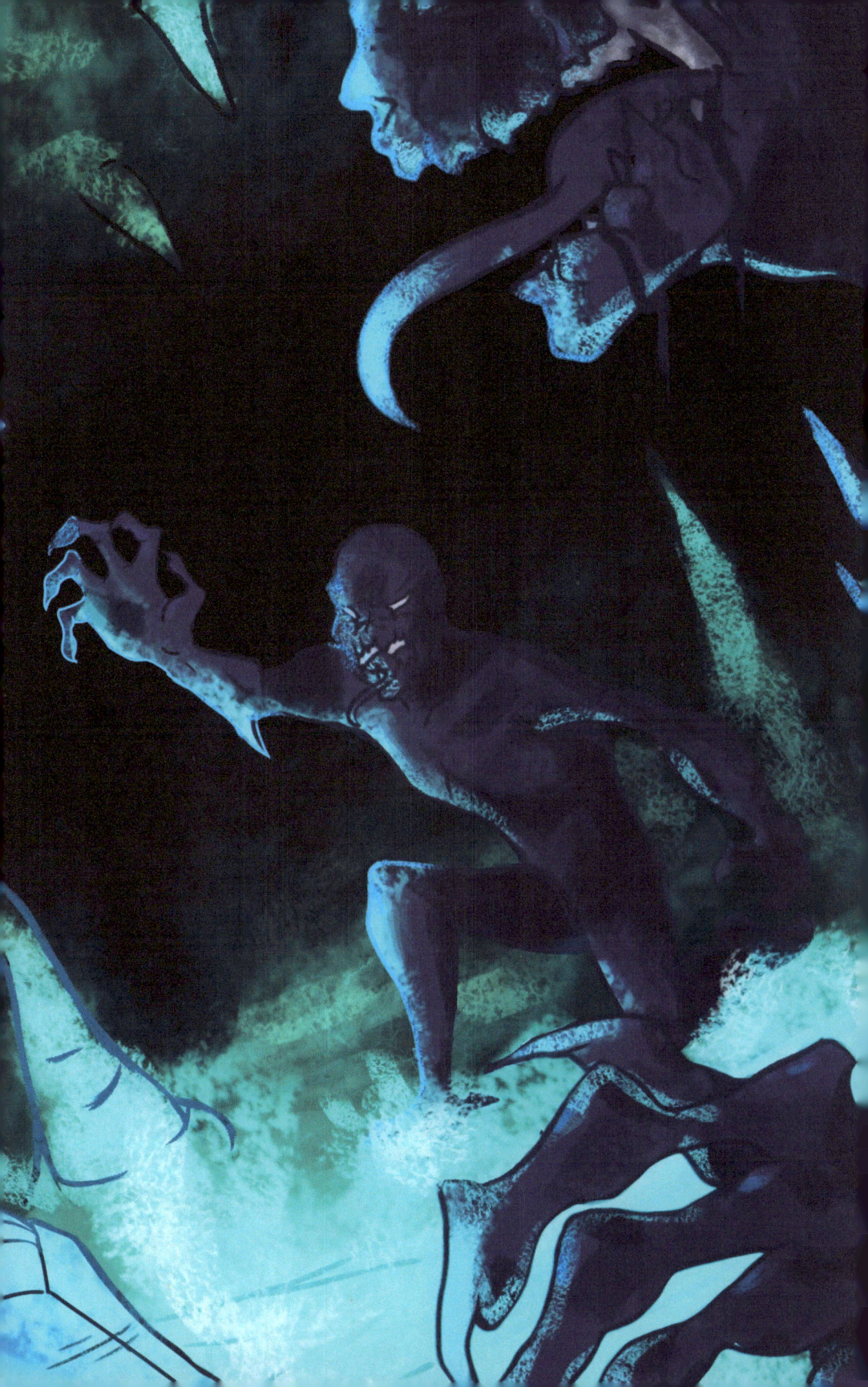

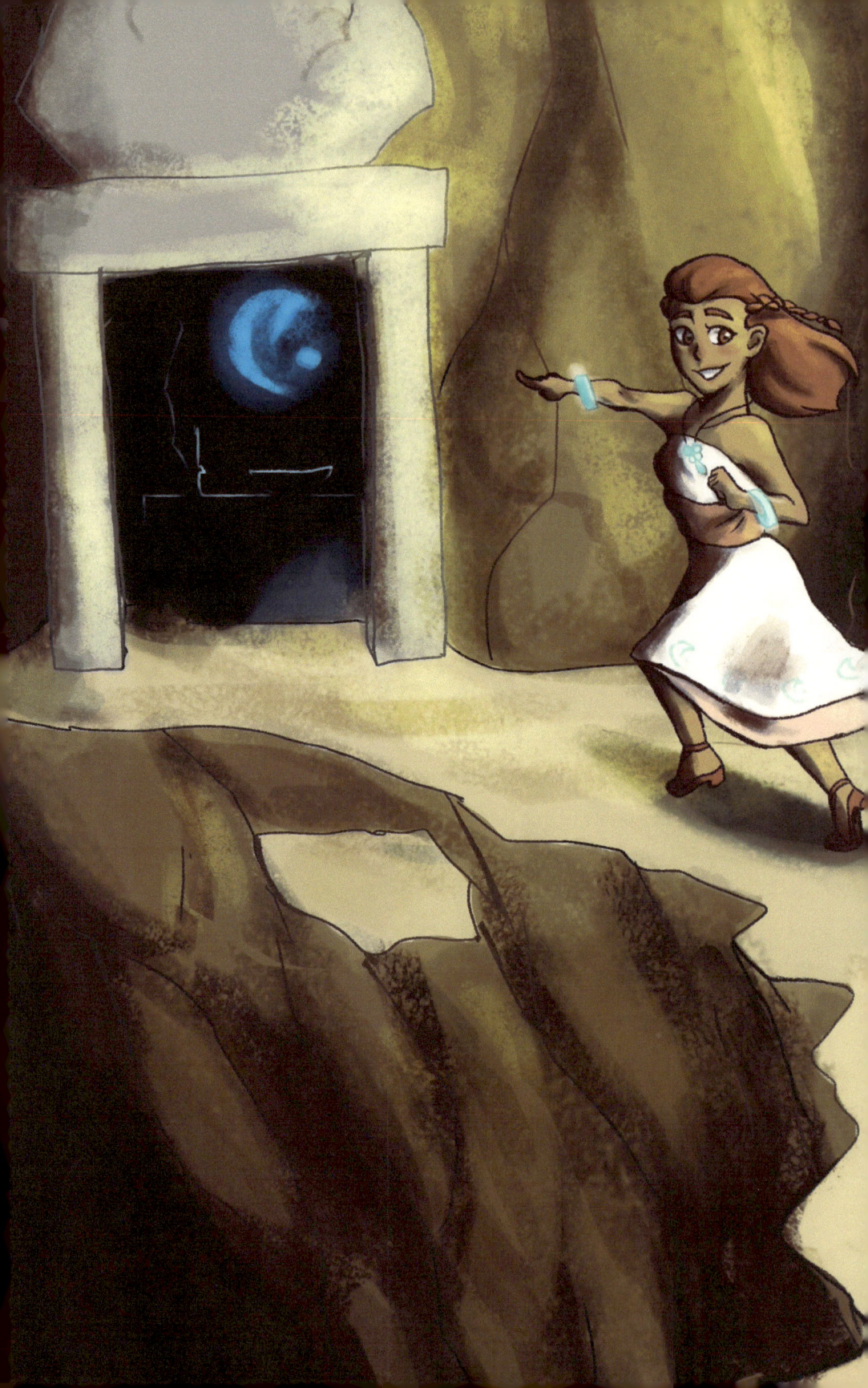

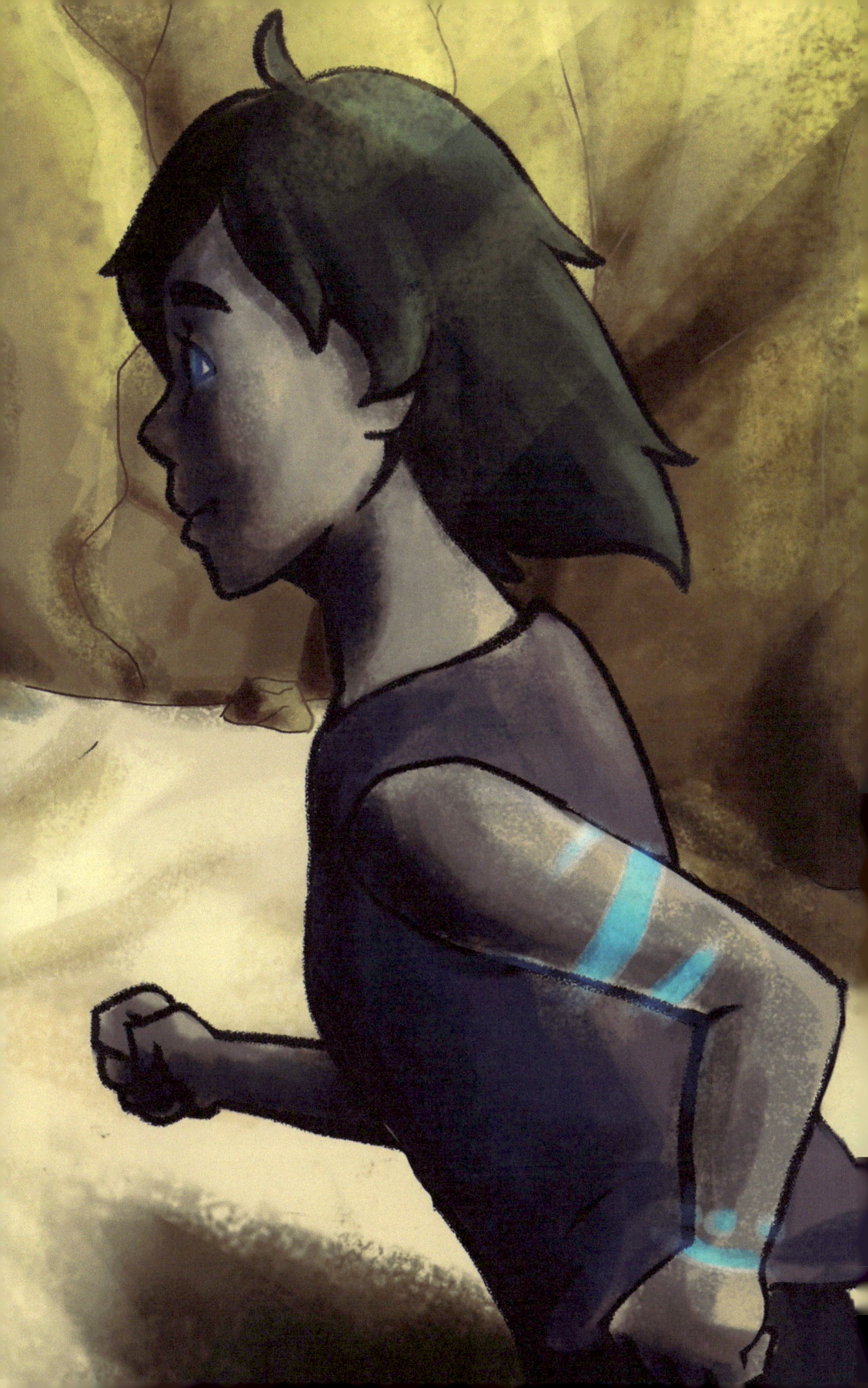

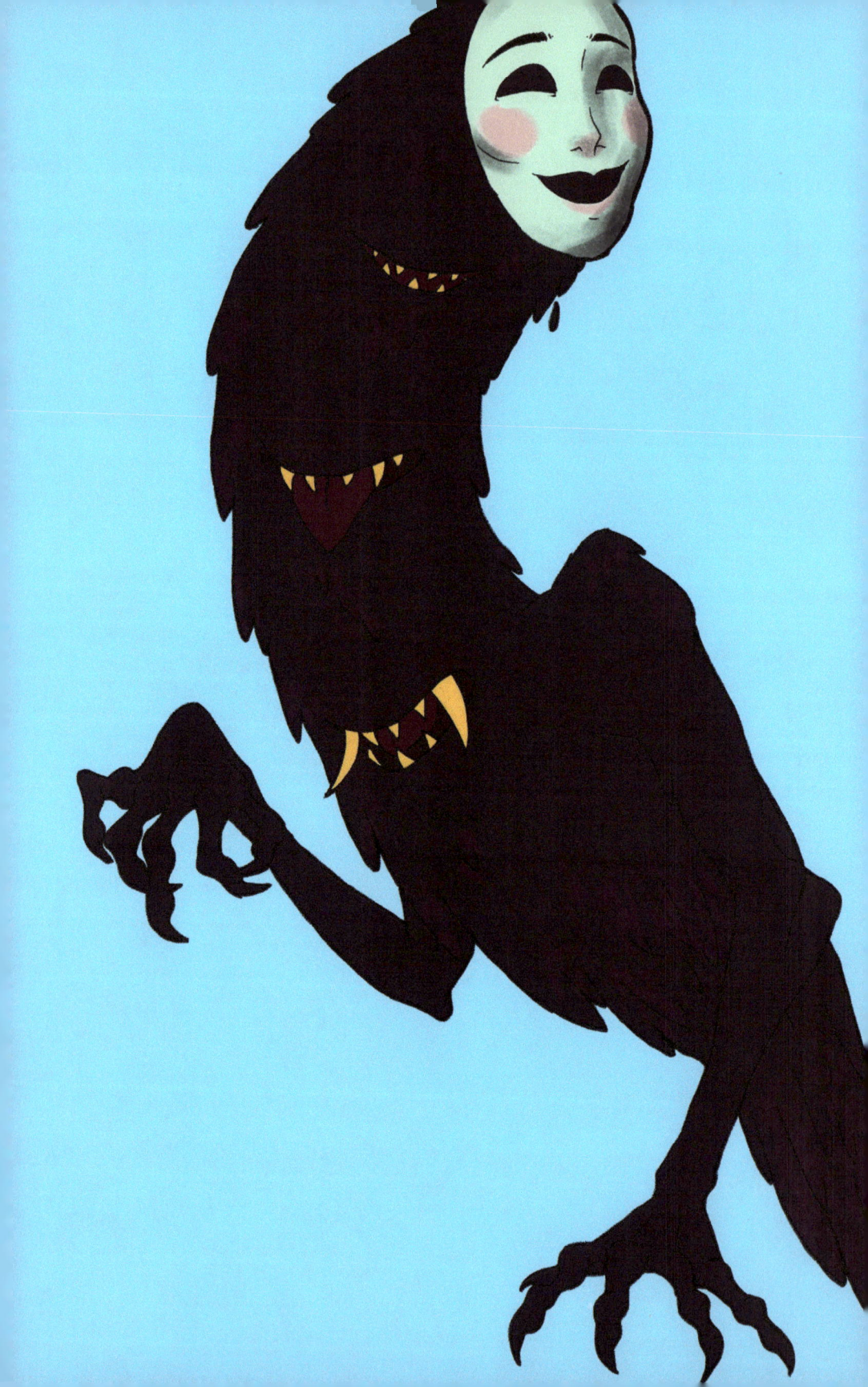

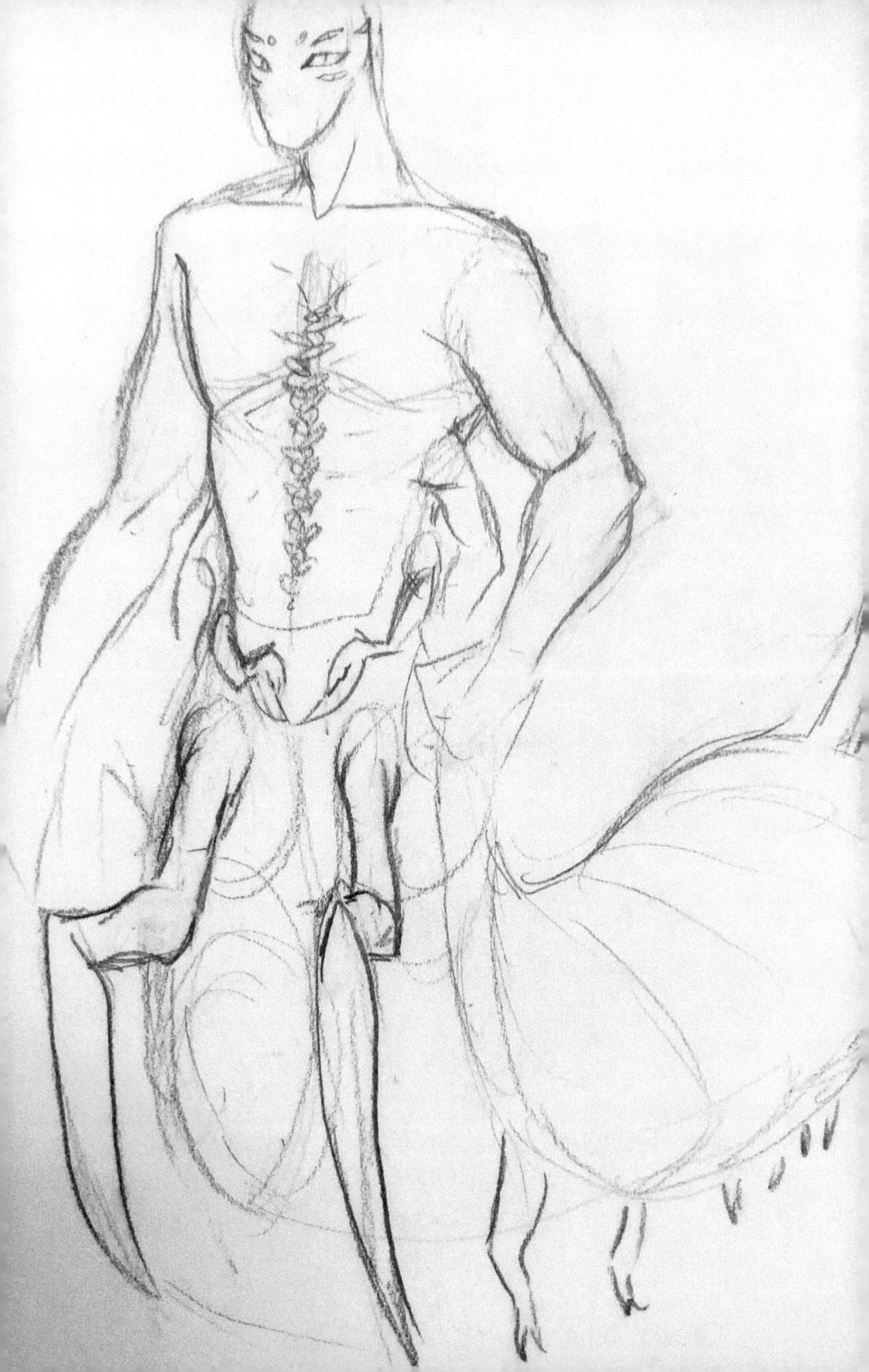

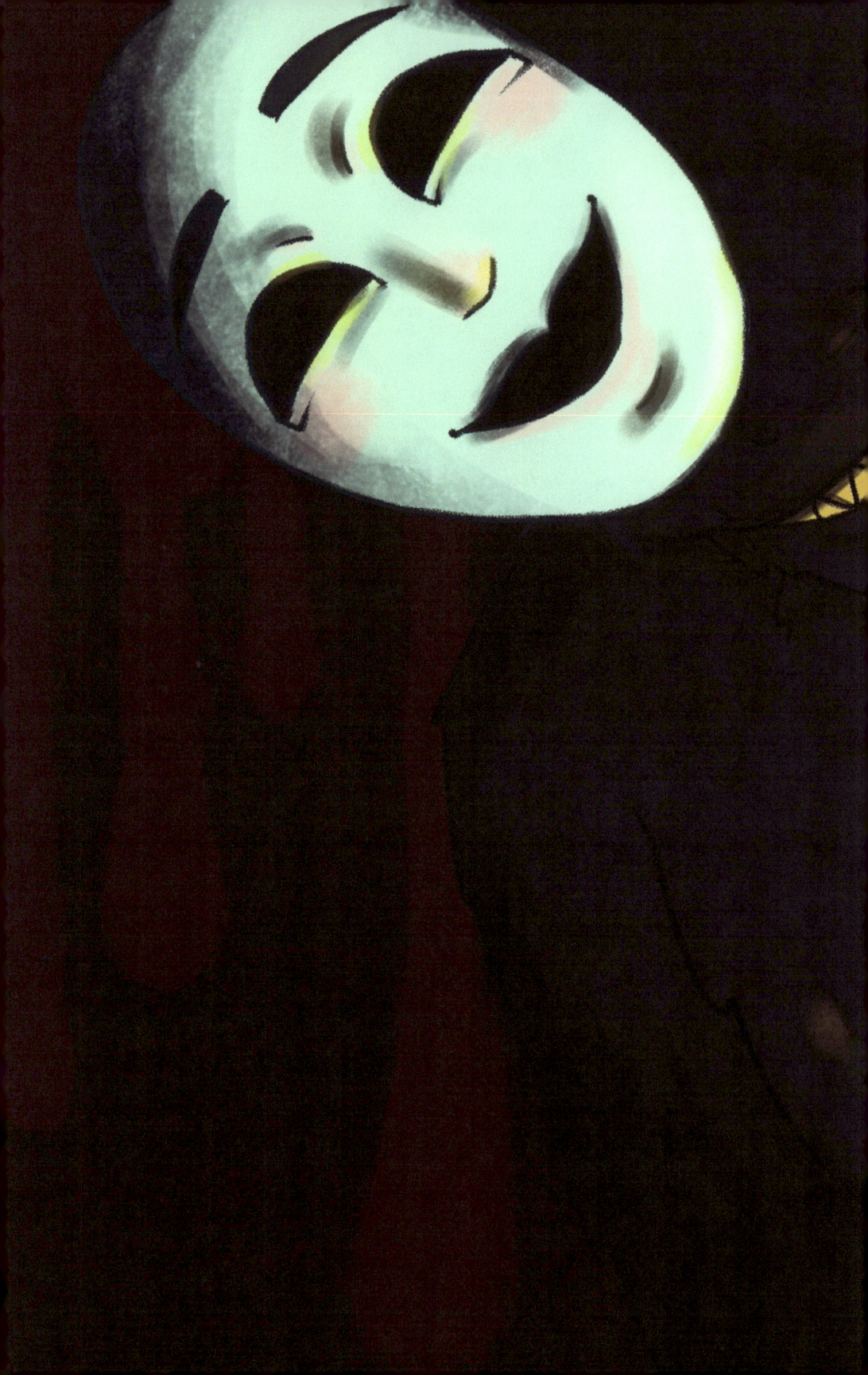

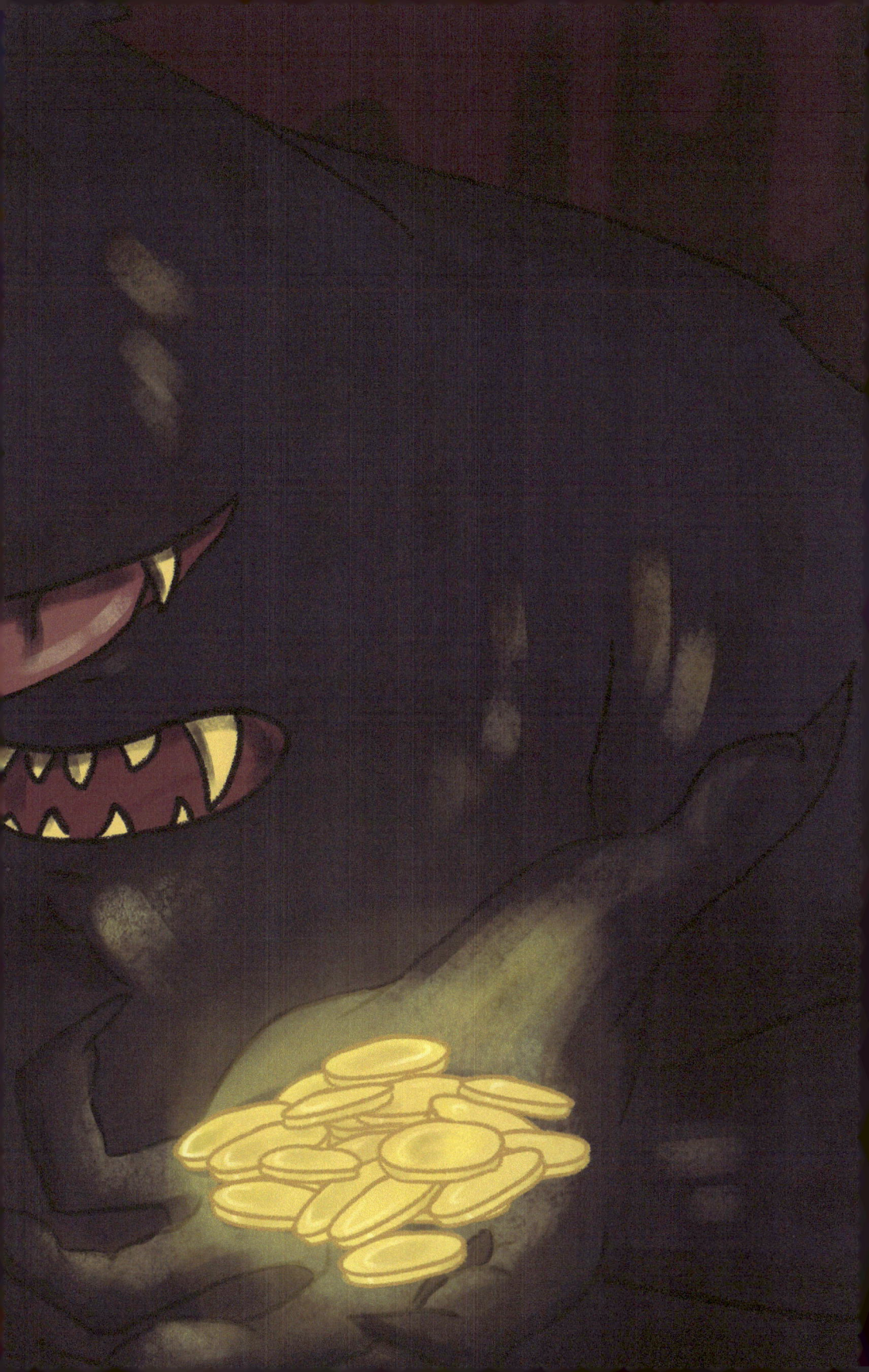

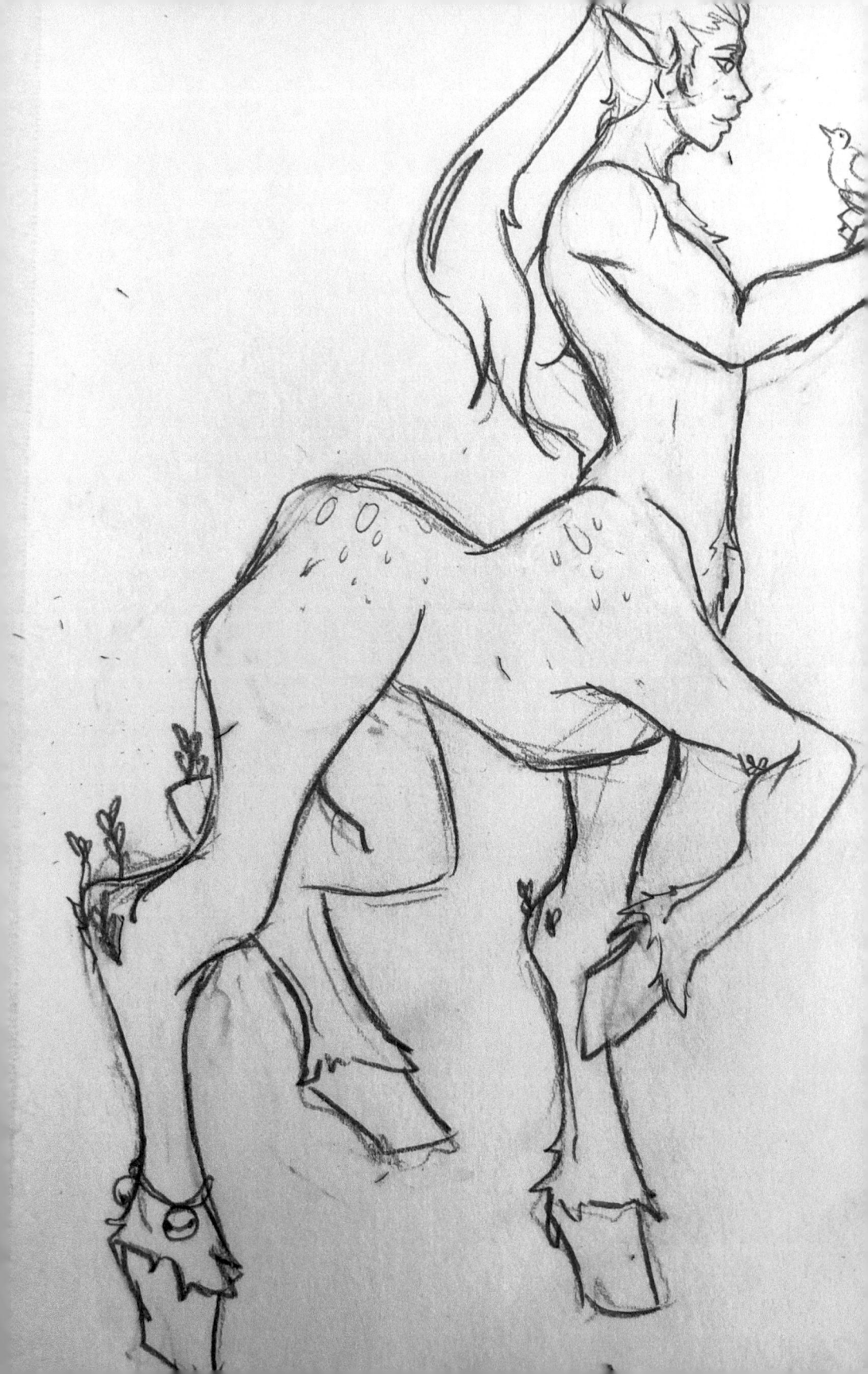

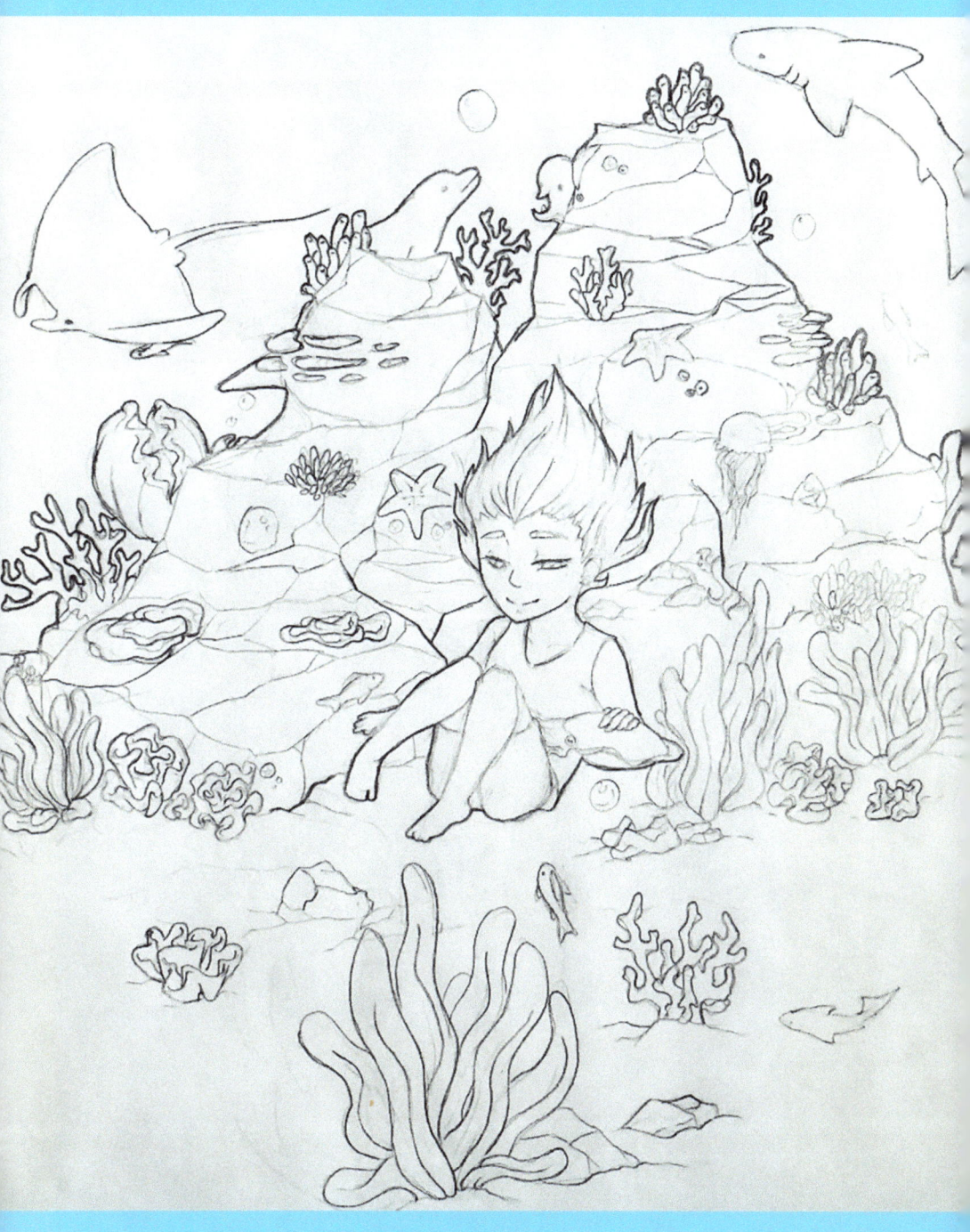

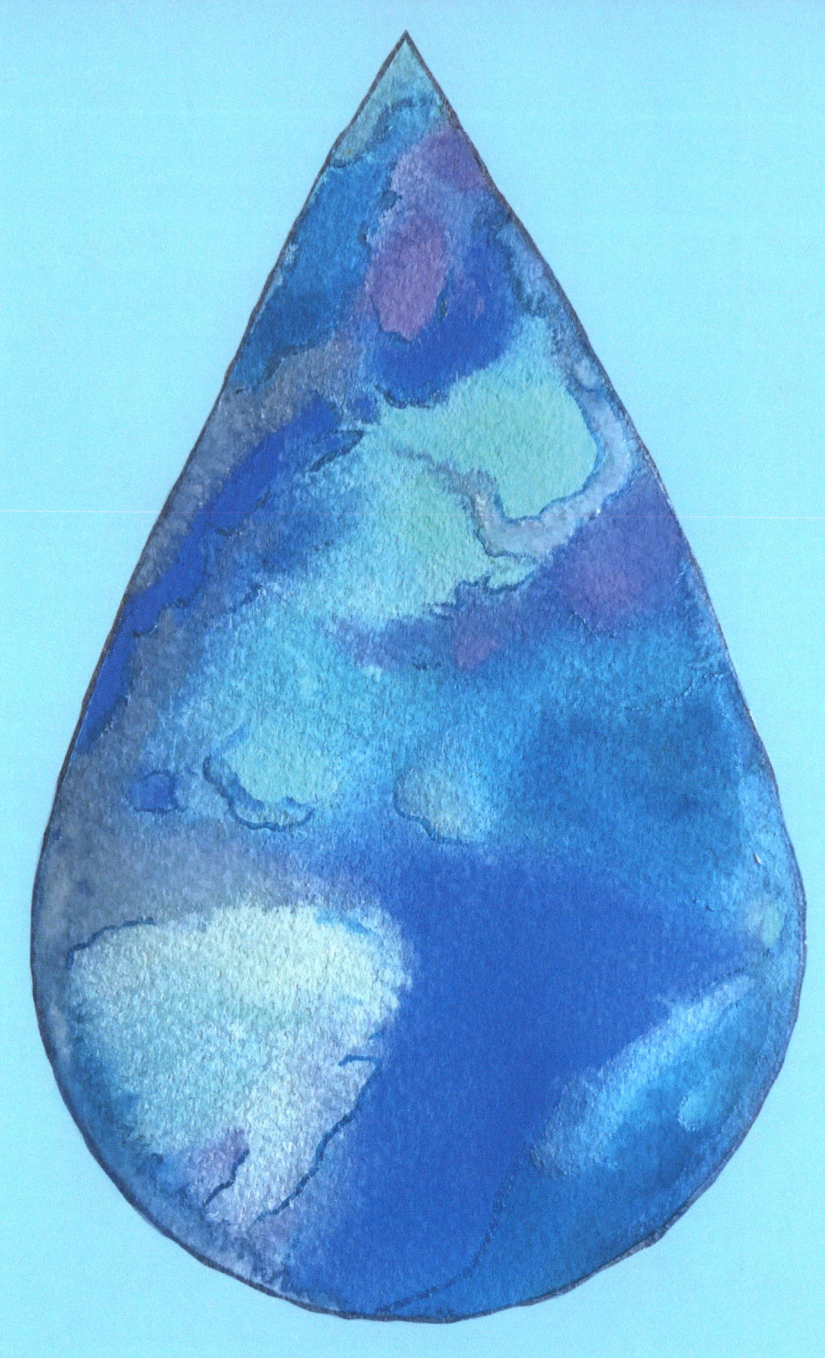

Wanna contact me?
@briannahp_art
briannahpetersen@gmail.com
briannapetersen.myportfolio.com

www.ingramcontent.com/pod-product-compliance
Lightning Source LLC
Chambersburg PA
CBHW040338220526
45473CB00009B/2722